Understanding the
TAROT

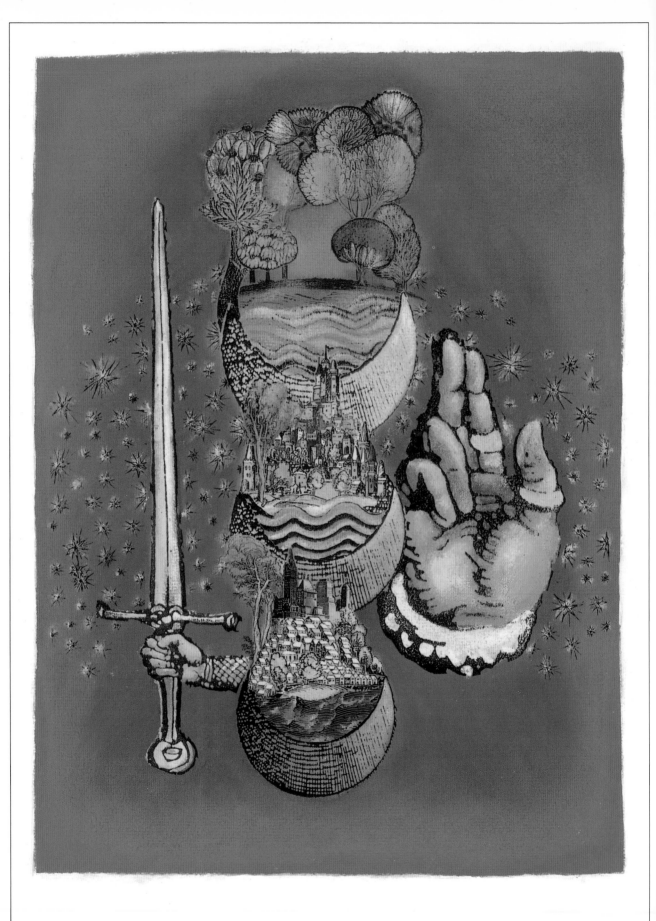

Understanding the
TAROT

— *A personal teaching guide* —

JULIET SHARMAN-BURKE

RIDER

London • Sydney • Auckland • Johannesburg

To my family, with love and thanks for their support

First published in Great Britain in 1998 by Rider,
an imprint of Ebury Press, Random House,
20 Vauxhall Bridge Road
London SW1V 2SA.

www.randomhouse.co.uk

Random House UK Limited Reg. No. 954009

A CIP catalogue record for this book is available from the British Library

ISBN 0-7126-7104-8

1 3 5 7 9 10 8 6 4 2

AN EDDISON•SADD EDITION
Edited, designed and produced by
Eddison Sadd Editions Limited
St Chad's House, 148 King's Cross Road
London WC1X 9DH

Phototypeset in Aldus and BernhardModern BT using QuarkXPress on Apple Macintosh
Origination by C.H. Colour Scan SDN BHD, Kuala Lumpur, Malaysia
Printed by C & C Offset Printing Co. Ltd, Hong Kong

CONTENTS

CHAPTER ONE

INTRODUCTION TO THE TAROT AND ITS USES

The tarot consists of seventy-eight cards – twenty-two of the Major Arcana and fifty-six of the Minor Arcana. Major Arcana means 'greater secrets' and its cards are recognizable as important archetypes, such as The Fool, The Hermit and The Sun. The Minor Arcana will probably seem familiar as it is divided into four suits rather like our modern playing cards. The suits, however, have different names – Cups, Wands, Swords and Pentacles – and each has an extra court card, the Page. The aim of this book is to study these cards, examining in depth both the divinatory meanings and the imagery of different decks. We will consider the mythology and symbolism of each card and see how each image reflects its meaning. This chapter will deal with some of the possible origins of the tarot, taking a brief look at its history, moving on to explore some of the uses to which the tarot can be put. We will then use twelve popular decks to discuss the different styles and make comparisons between them, finally suggesting various ways to familiarize yourself with the images.

DISCOVERING THE TAROT

Learning to read the tarot cards from a book can be difficult, and nothing beats a personal tutor–student relationship. Of course not everyone can attend lessons in person, so I have tried to do the next-best thing by repeating some of the conversations I have had with students, citing their questions and my comments, to make your learning experience more personal. All the conversations used throughout this book arose during actual teaching sessions.

The Origins of the Tarot

Although there are a great many perfectly feasible theories around as to the origins of the tarot, they nonetheless remain theories. The only thing we know for certain is that the tarot cards were documented in Italy, France and Germany by the second half of the fourteenth century; but how they came into existence, who designed them and for what purpose, is still largely a mystery.

It does, however, seem likely that the images on the tarot formed part of a memory system. The 'art of memory' was invented by the ancient Greeks and was based on a technique of impressing images on the mind and associating information with them. When the information needed to be recalled, a glance at the image was all that was required for the information 'filed' under it to unfold automatically. This technique was inherited by the Romans, and was thus passed into the European tradition. It could be used simply as an aid in memorizing texts or long passages, but could also work as a pictorial aid to meditation (*see Using the Tarot for Meditation, page 15*).

Memory systems in the Renaissance became linked with magical talismans or amulets which were thought to invoke a sense of a particular power at work in life on a great many levels. This was a kind of meditation, often involving a sort of spiritual ladder upon which the initiate could climb to reach higher levels of consciousness and be rewarded with insight into the world of the gods.

The images of pagan deities which often appear on the tarot symbolize the great laws at work through the whole of creation. The idea was that, by meditating on such images, a 'memory' of the divine world of the soul could be restored. This, in turn, would raise individual consciousness from the mundane or material world and reconnect the individual with the divine source of life.

STUDENT *I have heard that the tarot and the Cabbalistic Tree of Life are connected.*

JULIET No hard historical evidence has been found categorically connecting the tarot and the Cabbala; and no link has been found between the twenty-two Major Arcana cards, the twenty-two letters of the Hebrew alphabet, or the twenty-two paths on the Cabbalistic Tree of Life. However, the coincidences do seem hard to ignore.

Putting it as briefly as possible, Cabbala is a mixture of medieval mysticism, Gnosticism and Spanish Judaism. The Tree of Life is a mystical explanation of how the universe came to existence. The Cabbala teaches that creation was accomplished through a series of divine emanations in which God, the unmanifest, wished to behold himself, and so overflowed into manifestation, creating the first sphere of existence known as Kether, or the Crown. When this sphere was complete, the divine power overflowed again and created the next sphere down, known as Hokmah, or Wisdom, and so on until ten spheres, or sephiroth, were created. The Tree, with its roots in the earth and the tips of its branches in the heavens, provides a spiritual ladder by which God can reach man and man can reach God.

Each letter of the Hebrew alphabet signifies a special spiritual power to the Cabbalist and each letter has a connection with a 'path' on the Tree of Life (*see opposite*). Yet it was not until the nineteenth century – when a Frenchman known as

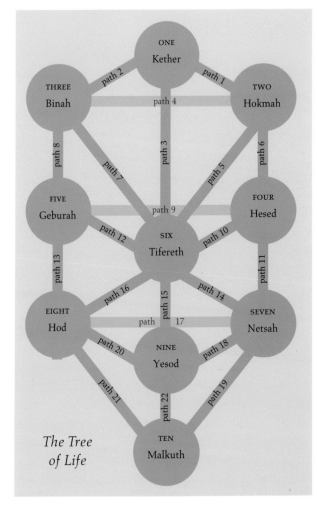

The Tree of Life

Middle Ages known as Trumps or Triumphs is still played in Europe today. The tarot has also been used by occultists as a means of improving communications with the gods or spirit world; and it has been used as a means of divination or fortune-telling. The distinction made between divination and fortune-telling by older-generation occultists (many of whom were men) seems to have been biased rather heavily by the social attitudes of the times. They maintained that 'divination' was a serious-minded effort to penetrate mystery by an elite group of the initiated, while 'fortune-telling' was merely a shoddy way of making money, which catered particularly to 'women and the lower classes'!

STUDENT | *So what is your objective when using the tarot?*

JULIET | My personal objective when reading the tarot is not to find out 'what is going to happen in the future', but rather to try to understand the current rhythms and patterns at work, so that life can be worked *with* rather than *against*. There are times for everything in life, times for beginnings and endings, times for planting, growing and reaping. The most helpful thing, I feel, is to understand and interpret the prevailing life energy so you can work with it.

Rather than tell fortunes, which tend to involve predictions of the 'you-will-cross-water-with-a-dark-stranger-who-wishes-you-ill' variety, my aim is to 'divine'. Divination is an attempt to acquire knowledge of the past, present or future through insight and intuition; and it is possible to gain access to the unconscious mind which 'knows' through the images of the tarot. Understanding patterns in life which are archetypal and being able to read them from the card images is the key to revealing what is happening beneath the surface. This is why it is not enough just to learn the meaning of each card and repeat it mechanically – the cards must be made to 'speak'. The images need to be understood and allowed to reveal themselves to the reader by a process of associations which work at a deep level.

Eliphas Levi pronounced that he had 'discovered' a link between the cards of the Major Arcana, the paths of the Cabbalistic Tree of Life and the letters of the Hebrew alphabet – that the links were studied, documented and taken seriously. In addition, the ten sephiroth may have a connection to the cards Ace to Ten in the Minor Arcana, and the four levels which exist in each sephiroth may be linked to the four court cards and the four suits. You will see the Tree of Life again as a spread in Chapter Four (*see page 123*); if you wish to learn more about this area of the tarot, please refer to the Further Reading on page 124.

The Uses of the Tarot

We do not know who invented the tarot or for what purpose. In its long history it has been used in many and various ways. One of its uses was as a game; and, indeed, the game devised in the

SELECTING YOUR DECK

The first thing you must do is spend time selecting a tarot deck of your own. It is not good enough to work with a deck just because your aunt gave it to you last Christmas, unless of course it happens to have great appeal for you. Ideally you should choose a deck yourself and, if you want to stick to an old tradition of divination, you should not haggle over the price! The most important thing is to choose a deck you really like, because once you have started to work with a deck, it is difficult to change, for reasons you will understand more fully as you progress.

To help in this choice I will introduce a varied range of tarot decks to give you an idea of the wide selection of styles, designs and imagery available. Nevertheless, the decks described here can, necessarily, only form a relatively small sample, bearing in mind the many decks on the market. It is a good idea to visit a specialist shop – the more decks you have to choose from the better, and there is certainly no shortage of choice!

Prior to 1970, the decks most commonly used were the Cary-Yale Visconti, the Marseilles, the 1JJ Swiss and the Rider-Waite. Since then, however, interest in tarot has increased steadily, and currently you can choose from a bewildering array ranging from cultural, story-telling, psychological, astrological, esoteric and women's tarots, to a cat-people tarot, a herbal tarot, a numerological tarot, a Native-american tarot, an Eskimo tarot and a Shakespeare tarot – and still many, many more.

For the purposes of discussion and illustration in this book, I have selected decks that are readily available to introduce a variety of cultures, styles, ages and traditions. Among the old decks are the Cary-Yale Visconti Tarocchi (Italian), the Tarot de Marseilles (French) and the 1JJ Swiss Tarot. The Rider-Waite Tarot (British), the most popular twentieth-century deck, was created in 1910 and was the first to use pictorial pip cards (cards Ace to Ten) for the Minor Arcana. The Tarot of the Witches (British) and the Morgan-Greer Tarot (American) were designed in the 1970s. Decks which pick up themes from different cultural or mythological backgrounds are El Gran Tarot Esoterico (Spanish), the Mythic Tarot (Greek mythology), the Norse Tarot (Viking sagas), the Russian Tarot of St Petersburg, the Ukiyoe Tarot (Japanese) and the Haindl Tarot (multi-cultural) – all designed in the 1970s and 1980s.

My aim in selecting these decks is to offer contrasting imagery rather than to recommend any one in particular, or to discount the many other decks available. The most crucial factor is to choose pictures that have a strong appeal for you personally. You must like the style, colour and spirit of the imagery. The symbolism must stimulate a strong personal preference and the essence of the cards must attract you because, in order to work with the tarot effectively, the images must impress themselves on your mind.

Choosing your deck is obviously a matter of taste and each deck has its merits; but in order to give you some guidelines, you might like to consider some of these factors. For instance, if you prefer the antique and strictly traditional, the Visconti, Swiss and Marseilles decks would have the advantage. Of course, if you like the elegant economy of line and things Japanese in general, the Ukiyoe Tarot might suit you. If you are familiar with or drawn towards classical Greek mythology, you might feel at home with the Mythic Tarot. For richness of design and depth of detail, the Rider-Waite, the Morgan-Greer or the Russian decks might appeal. On the other hand, if you are interested in Viking sagas and like the added information of the runes, it would be as well to consider the Norse Tarot. If you prefer a surrealist style, you might choose the Tarot of the Witches. Alternatively, if you are looking for a break from traditional imagery into something very dream-like, try the Haindl Tarot.

The Cary-Yale Visconti Tarocchi

Among the earliest-known tarot cards were those created for the Visconti-Sforza family, believed to have been painted in fifteenth-century Italy. Most of the original cards of the Cary-Yale Visconti Tarot are reproduced from the Cary Collection of Playing Cards, USA. In 1983, additional cards were repainted to replace the missing ones. The original Visconti deck included cards for Faith, Hope and Charity (which do not normally appear in the tarot and do not appear in the deck currently available) making up the seven virtues – the fo[...]rtues appear in the form of Justice, Strength, Tem[...]Hermit. Its Minor Arcana contains an extra fema[...]suit, so each contains sixteen cards instead of t[...] Ace to Ten plus four court cards. None of its pi[...]he hand-painted cards of this ancient deck are [...]ed and detailed. They echo the style of the time, [...] of the Visconti family, am[...]ed coiled viper, a dove bear[...]with the motto 'A bon dro[...]g the right'), a crown and the im[...]y Roman Empire.

The style of the Swiss deck (far left) is simpler than the Visconti (above), lacking the gold-leaf and many ornamentations.

The 1[...]

This deck [...]ating back perhaps to 1680 or e[...]rs to the cards of Juno and Jupi[...]alents of the Greek deities H[...]mes were changed to 'the Pope[...]ater decks to appease the Church. The style of the illustrations is distinctly classical and the colours are clear and bright. The pip cards are not pictorial.

Le Tarot de Marseilles

Dating back to circa 1751, the Marseilles deck has reproduced original tarot woodcut designs using simple primary colours. The result, although crude, is nevertheless striking and effective. Like the Visconti and the 1JJ Swiss, this deck does not use pictures on the Minor Arcana.

LE · MAT

The Rider-Waite Tarot

This British deck was drawn by Pamela Colman-Smith under the strict supervision of Arthur Edward Waite in 1910. These evocative and beautiful representations, with their clear and descriptive imagery, inspired many other designers to depart from tradition and produce different styles of decks. It was the first deck to use pictorial pip cards.

THE FOOL

The Marseilles deck (above) has a traditional, naive charm, while the Rider-Waite deck (left) represented a new trend in design.

THE FOOL.

The Tarot of the Witches

This deck was designed in 1974 by Fergus Hall, a Scottish artist. You may, perhaps, recognize it from the James Bond 007 film *Live and Let Die* in which it was featured. The figures are stylized and striking, with an almost comical air about them, and the imagery is surreal and dreamlike using clear and vibrant colours. The Minor Arcana cards are not pictorial but use only the symbols of the Cups, Wands, Swords and Pentacles.

El Gran Tarot Esoterico

El Gran Tarot Esoterico, or 'The Great Esoteric Tarot', was drawn by Luis Pena Longa in 1976 under the direction of Maritxu Guler, a man known as 'the Good Sorcerer', who lived in the Pyrenees near San Sebastian, Spain. The cards are bold and evocative with stunning colours and a somewhat primitive style. Each of the Major Arcana has been assigned a Hebrew letter and some of the cards bear signs of the zodiac, although the pip cards are not pictorial.

The cards of the Witches deck are dramatic in design using distorted bodies with little heads and large shoulders.

The style of imagery in the Great Esoteric deck (right) is not unlike the woodcut effect of the Marseilles deck, and the colours are very vivid.

The Morgan-Greer Tarot

The Morgan-Greer deck was drawn using beautiful rich colours by William Greer in 1979 under the direction of Lloyd Morgan. The deck draws much of its imagery and symbolism from the earlier Rider-Waite deck, although its figures are much larger and more dramatic in comparison. The pip cards are all pictorial.

The Ukiyoe Tarot

In 1982 Stuart Kaplan supervised the creation of this deck by Koji Furuta. It reflects the Ukiyoe-style art of the seventeenth- and eighteenth-century Edo period of Japan. This unusual deck combines traditional tarot imagery with Japanese mythology, customs and art. Many of the cards depict figures from Japanese folk tales with Buddhist themes. The pip cards are not pictorial.

The deep colours and detailed imagery of the Morgan-Greer deck (above left) are in distinct contrast to the clear simple lines and delicate colours of the Ukiyoe deck (right), which reflects the traditional Japanese style.

THE FOOL

the Fool

The Mythic Tarot

Designed by Liz Greene and Juliet Sharman-Burke, this deck was drawn by Tricia Newell in 1985. Greek myths have been assigned to each card and the stories are intended to be used as a springboard from which to enrich an understanding of the psychological uses the tarot can be put to. Each of the Major Arcana depicts a god or goddess whose myth or character in some way reflects the card's meaning. The pips are pictorial and a myth runs through each suit to aid the learning process.

The detailed illustrations of the Mythic Tarot (above left) are rich in both colour and symbolism.

The finely drawn images of the Norse deck (above) use soft and subtle hues to capture the magic of Viking mythology.

The Norse Tarot

These cards were designed and drawn in 1989 by Clive Barrett – who also wrote the accompanying book – using Viking history, its legends, gods and myths, as a reference for the images. Each Major Arcana card has been assigned a rune and the pips are all pictorial. In the court cards, the Prince corresponds to the Page and the Princess to the Knight.

The Russian Tarot of St Petersburg

Painted by Yury Shakov, who died in 1989, this exquisite tarot deck was his final commissioned work. Russian miniature painting is a highly specialized, extremely exacting form of art. The paintings were done to exact size, sometimes using a paintbrush with only a single hair. The colours are vivid and striking against a black background. The pip cards are not pictorial.

The Haindl Tarot

This unique deck was created by Herman Haindl over many years and published in 1990; the accompanying book was written by his friend and tarot expert, Rachel Pollack. The cards are fascinating, powerful and dreamlike, with soft muted colours blending into fantastic imagery. Instead of the traditional King, Queen, Knight and Page of the court cards, the Haindl deck uses Mother, Father, Daughter and Son, respectively. The court cards also use myths from different continents: Asia (fire), Africa (air), Europe (water) and America (earth).

The Haindl deck (right) blends spiritual traditions from many different cultures, using runes, astrological symbolism, Hebrew letters and I Ching hexagrams.

0

The Fool

The fine details in the Russian deck (above) are set off by a black background and rich oval borders reminiscent of Imperial Fabergé eggs.

HOW TO FAMILIARIZE YOURSELF WITH THE CARD IMAGES

Once you have chosen a deck which appeals to your sense of colour, style and imagery, the next step is to familiarize yourself thoroughly with your cards. Study each image carefully in turn, making notes of the first impressions you have of each one. What does the image evoke in you? Does it feel comforting, alarming, inviting, repulsive? You might like to make up some worksheets for yourself and use them to make notes of your own ideas about each card before you start reading the section on their meanings in Chapters Two and Three. It is fun to check your personal interpretations against those offered in the book, so you can notice the similarities or differences between them.

A traditional method of getting to know your cards is to select a different card each night and study it carefully before you fall asleep, tucking the chosen card under your pillow. Let the image imprint itself on your mind and then allow your unconscious to take over. This process often stimulates dreams and fantasies which all develop and deepen your inner understanding of the cards.

The aim is for you to feel easy and comfortable with the cards: they should feel as familiar to you as old friends. It will take time and effort to decipher the symbols and images of the tarot, just as it took time and effort to learn to decipher letters and words when you learned to read. But, if you take the trouble to stay with the learning process, reading the cards will prove as rewarding as reading a book.

Sense Associations

Getting to know your cards is a very personal process and involves your spending time and trouble in forming your own string of associations to each one. Ideally you should involve all your senses in the process. The aim of the following exercise is to form a chain of associations which relate to each of the Major Arcana cards. Link a colour, a tune, a scent, a sound, a sensation and anything else you like, even a taste, in an associative chain so that you only have to pick up one thread of the chain for the rest to unfold quite naturally in your mind.

Let us try an example. Take The Sun card and look hard at the image. Let associations swim to the forefront of your mind. Jot down any ideas that emerge instantly, working quickly and instinctively. Now start your association chain. Think of a piece of music, any tune or song which could fit with your feelings about the sun. Depending on your taste, you might link a popular song, like 'Here Comes the Sun', or you might prefer a piece of classical music – it really does not matter what you choose as long it means something to you. Next, try choosing a fragrance which you could connect with the solar image. Again, anything you like – an example might be the smell of oranges, which are traditionally solar fruit, or maybe the scent of orange blossom. You could add a plant or flower to your list of associations, perhaps sunflowers, heliotrope or marigolds, all said to be solar plants because they 'follow' the sun with their heads. You might choose to work with The Sun card on a Sunday – the day of the sun – or use the hours of the day when the sun is at its most potent – at dawn, midday or sunset. The sun colours might be yellow, red or orange, and you might choose gold or brass as an associated metal. Your final chain could be something like: 'Here comes the Sun', oranges, heliotrope, Sunday, midday, red, gold. So, if you think of one of the string, say, heliotrope, the rest of the chain will unfold quite naturally. Of course, the selection of associations is entirely up to you. The object of the exercise is to link together a number of associations to, in this example, solar imagery in general. So let your imagination go wild within the general outline of imagery the card offers you to work with.

STUDENT *Can you use your associations in readings or are they just to familiarize yourself with the essence of the card?*

JULIET It works like this: if you feel really familiar with each card it automatically enriches your capacity to read the tarot more fluently. Your associations will help your ability to intuitively understand the cards better and will thus give you more confidence when reading them. You will not have to learn the meanings of all seventy-eight cards by rote and you will not have to keep referring to the book to see what a card 'means'. I suggest you do the sense associations exercise for each card using your own, as well as traditional, associations, noting the differences that arise.

STUDENT *I tried that exercise with The Moon and my associations were: lily, silver, silk, white, Moonlight Sonata, jasmine, ice, crystal. I have been following the lunar phases, too, and try to be aware of the difference between new-moon and full-moon energy. I make a point of reflecting on The Moon card at night whereas I definitely feel inclined to study The Sun card in daylight. I think it really helps to build up a wide range of feelings around each card.*

JULIET Good. It is obvious that the chain of associations you develop for each card will be different from the next person's, but the important thing is the special value with which the tarot image will be impressed on your mind after you have spent this time and effort on it. Keep a notepad or folder for recording such exercises with all the Major Arcana. Add any particular thoughts you have on anything connected to a particular card. It will form part of an invaluable record of your studies.

Using the Tarot for Meditation

STUDENT *Can you use the tarot as an aid to meditation?*

JULIET Yes, you can simply use the cards as a focus for general guided daydream work or you can use the images as a focus to guide you on a particular situation you may be encountering. For instance, if you have a dilemma about relationships, or about choices or directions to take, try focusing on The Lovers. If you are struggling with depression or anxiety, try reflecting on The Moon. If you need a bit of good cheer and optimism, contemplate The Sun. The reasons I am suggesting these cards will become clearer when we examine the Major Arcana in detail later on (*see Chapter Two*).

To follow a guided daydream exercise, set aside a quiet hour for yourself when you will not be disturbed. Turn the phone off. Sit or lie down in a comfortable position, making sure you are warm and feel completely at ease. A few deep breaths in through the nose and out through the mouth should help to relax you. Now take the card you plan to work with and look at it closely. Allow the colours and imagery to impress themselves so deeply on your mind that even with closed eyes the image is as clear as when they are open. As soon as you are able to visualize the card clearly with your eyes closed, allow your imagination to take over. Let the image on the card become three dimensional and, if there is a figure on the card, try holding a conversation. Ask questions, listen to the answers and generally imagine the scene. When you have finished, close the exercise properly by allowing the figure to turn back into a two-dimensional image on the card again and then open your eyes. Afterwards make notes of the conversation and pay attention to all the feelings evoked during your imaginary meeting. Keep a diary or record of all such guided fantasy exercises, comparing the experiences you have with different cards. If you do this exercise carefully with each card a personal catalogue of great value can be gradually built up.

CHAPTER TWO

THE MAJOR ARCANA

We will now look at the Major Arcana in some detail. In order to give you an idea of the different imagery that various decks use, I have selected four different cards for each Major trump from the twelve decks featured. The divinatory meanings are standard and as close to traditional as possible, but obviously the pictorial imagery varies, often according to the approach of the author or designer.

The numbering of the decks is a subject which provokes much discussion and disagreement. The earliest Major trumps, such as the Visconti, bore no name or number, although many Italian fifteenth-century decks had Roman numerals at the top of each card, indicating some sort of sequence. The order has been switched around frequently over the ages, usually in an attempt to make the cards fit one theory or another. What the twenty-two trumps do seem to describe, however, are the archetypal stages of life which we all experience in our unique ways, described along the lines of myths and fairy tales and, indeed, Jungian psychology.

The journey through the tarot is the journey of The Fool, as we begin in childhood and experience education, signified by The Magician. The Empress and The Emperor are earthly parents, and The High Priestess and The Hierophant are spiritual parents. We all experience, too, the trials of adolescence, namely love and war, with The Lovers and The Chariot. The tests of adulthood follow with the four medieval virtues of Justice, Temperance, Strength and The Hermit (or Prudence). Then, half-way through the cycle, The Wheel of Fortune turns and we experience some change or loss, commonly identified today as a mid-life crisis. It evokes in us a need to change, find new direction, look inward – and this soul-searching is marked by The Hanged Man, Death, The Devil and The Tower. After our struggle with our own dark side, we are ready to encounter the higher principles in The Star, The Moon and The Sun, and our victory over darkness ultimately results in rebirth, in Judgement, and triumph, in The World. While this sequence is a psychological one and does not strictly follow the numbering of modern decks, it is a useful one to keep in mind as we examine the twenty-two Major Arcana cards.

THE FOOL

The beginning of a cycle or an adventure; a risk must be taken

The Fool is the only one of the Major trumps to have survived in our modern playing decks – it is the Joker, the 'wild' card exempt from normal rules. The Fool has the same 'wild' quality in the tarot deck because his card is unnumbered and he can fit at the beginning, the end or, indeed, anywhere along the procession of trumps. The Grand Esoteric and the Witches' decks both depict The Fool as a court jester while the Visconti deck shows him as a beggar. Waite images him in a more romantic light as a free-spirited traveller. On the Tree of Life, The Fool is path one, which connects Kether, the crown, with Hokmah, meaning wisdom.

THE FOOL .

In the Rider-Waite card the stick and bundle represent the masculine, the rose, the feminine, symbolizing potential unity through combination of opposites.

The Rider-Waite Tarot

In the Waite deck, The Fool is portrayed, as he often is in other decks, about to walk off the edge of a cliff. The risks involved in such rash or foolish impulses are necessary because the card reflects a need for change, or new experience. Over his shoulder the youth has tossed his bundle which represents past experiences that do not concern him at present. He holds a white rose which symbolizes innocence. Whether as a child at the moment of birth, full of promise and possibility, or as an adult searching afresh for new truth or meaning, he is discovering life for the first time. The dog prancing at the youth's feet signifies his mixed feelings about the journey, fear of the unknown combined with enthusiasm and zest for adventure. His hat of interwoven laurel leaves is a symbol of success, with the red feather reflecting desire.

The Cary-Yale Visconti Tarocchi

The Visconti Fool shows a tattered beggar with a bundle over his shoulder and a staff in hand. His simple shirt is white, symbolizing purity and innocence. The image of a beggar is of one who has nothing to lose but everything to gain: The Fool represents the beginning of a venture when all is still possible. Although this Fool is not as vibrant as the others, he is pictured with his eyes turned upwards, suggesting he is not fretting about what lies ahead: The Fool trusts in life and luck, even when things look bleak.

The Visconti card (right) shows six feathers poking from The Fool's hair; the feather was an emblem of truth and divine order in ancient Egypt.

El Gran Tarot Esoterico

This deck shows The Fool wearing a jester's cap with horns and ass's ears thought to derive from Dionysus, the 'Lord of Misrule'. Dionysus was a revolutionary god who overturned established rule and rebelled against the strictures of authority. Son of the mighty god Zeus and a mortal woman, Semele, he reflects the connection between the divine and natural world. Attacked by his wicked uncles, the Titans, who tore him to pieces and devoured him, Dionysus defeated death and was reborn in the underworld as the god of light and joy. He became associated with ecstasy and madness: his followers were given the gift of wine and his rituals were orgiastic and bizarre. The tarot Fool represents the wild spirit in each of us.

EL LOCO
300

| STUDENT | *Is The Fool connected with any other legendary figures?* |

| JULIET | Yes, several. One example is the Green Man of Spring, who led the springtime procession in various parts of Europe, dressed in |
leaves and branches. He represents the child of spring who succeeds the dead king of winter, reflecting the theme of defeating death and triumphant rebirth. Others are Egyptian Horus, Persian Mithra or Arthurian Parsival.

In the Esoteric card The Fool wears traditional jester's bells and carries a ripe maize symbolizing fertility.

The Tarot of the Witches

The Tarot of the Witches shows The Fool dressed as a court jester, again walking blindfold, over the edge of a hill. The wandering fools or court jesters, in whom some tarot writers see The Fool's origins, were those curious fellows whose mockery and pranks took their audiences out of their dreary mundane lives for a while, turning their world upside down. In this strange realm, the king could be mocked and jeered while the lowliest member of the court could, for a while at least, rule supreme. His clothes are multicoloured to reflect his muddled impulses which pull him in different ways. Red hearts adorn his cheeks, showing his naivety and inexperience. The dog, symbolizing animal instincts, rips at his brightly coloured trousers, but The Fool seems oblivious. He scatters coins carelessly, having no interest in worldly goods. It may even refer to the saying 'a fool and his money are easily parted', but of course it is also possible that The Fool knows the true value of money and is therefore not interested in it.

THE FOOL

Interpreting THE FOOL

The Fool reveals that old ways are outdated and suggests a powerful desire for change. A new chapter is starting and a willingness to take a leap into the unknown is required. There may be unexpected opportunities for adventure or escape. The Fool reflects the wish to seek out new ways of experiencing life which may seem unconventional and even appear 'foolish' to others. However, the desire to change is usually greater than the fear. This is a challenge not easily ignored, and it is likely that things will be ready to undergo changes.

The sun and moon appear together in the sky in the Witches card, showing the endless cycle of day and night, and suggesting opportunities are never-ending.

THE MAGICIAN

Creative initiative, skill and opportunities for new ventures

This card has had a number of titles over the years, ranging from The Magician in modern packs like the Morgan-Greer and the Norse decks, to the Juggler or Cobbler in the older Marseilles deck. His number is one, the number of creative power, and his path on the Tree of Life is two, connecting Kether, the crown, and Binah, meaning understanding or intelligence.

The Magician

The astrological glyph for Mercury in the Haindl card connects this card with Hermes. The rune Peorth means dice cup, which stands for gambling, speculation and potential wealth.

The Haindl Tarot

This deck combines many different esoteric traditions, including Native American, the Holy Grail, the I Ching, the Cabbala and the Runes, so its images are quite different from more traditional decks. The symbols in the foreground represent the four suits which, in turn, reflect different cultures. The Swords represent Egypt and the south; the Wands, India and the east; the Cups, Europe and the north; and finally the Stones (Pentacles or Coins in most other decks) represent America and the west. According to Haindl, the dark three-pointed headdress worn by The Magician is symbolic of the crowning power of the intellect. His right eye sees crystals, representing the capacity for perceiving pure forms of existence, while images from his left eye are faded by the darker emotions symbolized in the shadowy figure on the right of the card.

The Morgan-Greer Tarot

This deck shows The Magician clothed in a red cloak symbolizing his desire, and a white tunic reflecting the purity of his spirit. The red roses and white lilies in the foreground echo these qualities. He stands before a table upon which are laid out the Pentacle, Sword, Wand and Cup of the Minor Arcana suits. These represent the four astrological elements and the four Jungian psychological types as follows: Pentacles, earth, sensation; Swords, air, thinking; Wands, fire, intuition; and Cups, water, feeling. The Magician is associated with the versatile Greek messenger-god Hermes, who linked the worlds of gods and men, the divine and the human. Hermes, god of the mind and intelligence, was also the god of businessmen and thieves, which earned him the title of Trickster.

The Magician in the Morgan-Greer card (right) points one hand towards the heavens, and the other towards the earth, indicating his link between the gods and men.

I — THE MAGICIAN

the magician

STUDENT *What does the 'floating' figure eight above The Magician's head represent?*

JULIET Eight is the number of new life which is why many baptismal fonts in churches are octagonal. The lemniscate, or horizontal figure eight, above his head is the mathematical symbol for infinity, which represents eternal life. The Magician's belt is sometimes shown as a serpent devouring its own tail, which echoes the notion of life being never-ending and eternally self-renewing, as it feeds upon itself.

The Norse Tarot

The Norse deck, which takes its imagery from Viking sagas, depicts The Magician as Odin, the Norse god of wisdom, who was master of magic and wars. Odin was a fickle god and his followers knew that while they might be well rewarded if he were pleased, he could just as easily turn against them, granting battle victory to their opponents. This quality earned Odin the title of Trickster, like his Greek counterpart, Hermes. His all-seeing eye watched over the whole world and nothing escaped his penetrating gaze. Odin had two ravens, Hugin (thought) and Munin (memory), who spent their days searching the land for information to report back to their master each night, whispering to him all they had seen and heard.

The Norse card depicts Odin with his two wolves Geri and Freki, which he used as hunting dogs.

Le Tarot de Marseilles

The Marseilles deck shows The Magician, or Juggler, as a man wearing a hat with a brim shaped like the lemniscate, symbol of eternity. On his table lies an assortment of tools which indicate his numerous possibilities and talents. He holds up a rod which symbolizes the inspiration from divine sources that may translate into practical realities. In his other hand is a small ball which may represent the earth. He appears to be experimenting or working with the various objects which lie before him as though he is not content with the way things are and wants to seek out alternatives.

This card has also been connected with Prometheus who stole divine fire from the gods to give to man in order to make mankind more godlike. The parallel is that man achieves consciousness by 'stealing' from the unconscious and, in so doing, takes upon himself an aspect of the divine. The Magician links the unconscious and the conscious, the gods and men.

LE · BATELEUR

In the Marseilles card the plants at The Magician's feet reveal that the earth on which he stands is fertile and shows a potential for success.

Interpreting THE MAGICIAN

The Magician indicates potential for important new beginnings and a time for action and energy. This card reflects adaptability and versatility, suggesting that creative initiative and skills are plentiful. It indicates that reserves of power and dynamism are available, as symbolized by the four suit emblems, but the seeker must choose which direction to take – the mind (Swords); the imagination (Wands); the heart (Cups) or the body (Pentacles). The positive aspects of this card are strength of will while its negative side points to weakness of will or lack of nerve.

THE HIGH PRIESTESS

Wisdom, secrets to be revealed, and the development of intuition

The High Priestess has other titles such as The Female Pope in the Marseilles deck, which shows her in papal robes. The Rider-Waite and Norse decks show her with a crescent moon, connecting her with moon goddesses, Isis and Frigga. The Mythic Tarot depicts her as the virgin Persephone, goddess of the new moon. Her number is two, which symbolizes duality and balance or the opposing forces of conflict that develop from number one. Her path on the Tree of Life is three, linking Kether, the crown, with Tifereth meaning beauty.

THE HIGH PRIESTESS

The Mythic card portrays The High Priestess holding a pomegranate – the fruit of the dead and of marriage or conjugal love, because it is many-seeded.

The Mythic Tarot

The Mythic Tarot uses the virgin Persephone, daughter of the Greek earth mother Demeter, to portray The High Priestess. The virgin is a symbol of potential waiting to be fulfilled which, in the case of The High Priestess, is the treasure of the unconscious yet to be unfolded. According to myth, Persephone was alone picking flowers when she was abducted by Hades, lord of the underworld. In the dark land of the dead, she ate three pomegranate seeds which meant she was obliged to spend three months of the year with her dark husband. Persephone's world is like the unconscious mind, full of possibility but hidden from view. The High Priestess suggests that secrets of the unconscious will only be revealed at the appropriate time.

Le Tarot de Marseilles

The Marseilles deck uses an old title, La Papesse or The Female Pope. The image is of a woman in papal attire and may have been inspired by the bizarre medieval legend of Pope Joan, a girl from England who fell in love with a Benedictine monk and ran away with him disguised as a fellow monk. Sadly, their bliss was short, as her lover died. However, still disguised as a monk, Joan made her way to Rome and entered the priesthood. Being wise and pious she rose quickly in the church's hierarchy, became Cardinal Joannes, and eventually, as word of her wisdom and holiness spread, found herself elected to office of pope. Alas the story came to an abrupt end when, during the papal inauguration, she unexpectedly gave birth to a child on the steps of St Peter's and subsequently died.

The Marseilles card (right) depicts a woman dressed in papal robes and tiara, holding an open book symbolizing knowledge.

II

LA·PAPESSE

The Rider-Waite Tarot

The Rider-Waite deck shows a woman dressed in blue, with a white cross on her breast. This may indicate a link with the Virgin Mary in Christian tradition, while her horned headdress suggests a connection with the Egyptian goddess, Isis. On her lap she holds a scroll bearing the inscription 'TORA', which might mean 'natural law'; but the letters could also be rearranged to read 'TARO', a clue to the natural wisdom and law contained in the tarot itself. She sits between two pillars, one black, the other white, which bear the inscriptions 'B' and 'J'. They may recall the bronze columns, Boaz ('to establish') and Jachin ('in strength'), which stood at the threshold of the Temple in Jerusalem. Together they mean 'stability'. Behind the Priestess is a veil ornamented with pomegranates, the fruit particular to Persephone, Greek goddess of the underworld. This connects The High Priestess with the unconscious, and the water which can just be glimpsed behind the curtain suggests the hidden riches that lie concealed in the depths of the unconscious mind.

STUDENT	*Who was Isis?*

JULIET	Isis was the mother goddess of Egypt, sister and wife to the good king Osiris, who was killed by Set, his jealous brother. Isis searched

far and wide for her husband's body and, on finding it, performed magic to restore him to life for long enough to conceive a son, Horus, by him. Her mysteries were very popular as they promised life after death to those who were initiated into them.

The Rider-Waite card shows twin pillars which represent the balance of opposites – life and death, creation and destruction.

The Norse Tarot

The Norse deck has linked The High Priestess with Frigga, patroness of marriage. Her robe is white but behind her hangs a red cloak edged in black which represents the three phases of the moon and of womanhood – the new, full and old moons standing for the virgin, mother and old hag, respectively. Beyond her throne stand twin stones which represent duality. Frigga was a sky goddess whose clothes reflected the colours of the clouds. She had the gift of prophecy but seldom revealed predictions. She clutches her gown close, as if to conceal her insights and wisdom.

Interpreting THE HIGH PRIESTESS

This card reflects a heightened interest in the occult or esoteric studies. There is often a desire to learn more about the hidden world, and secrets may be revealed, although slowly and in their own good time. There is great yet unfulfilled potential, and the time is ripe for developing the feminine powers of intuition. A wise or insightful woman may prove to be influential. On the positive side, the seeker may benefit from looking at problems intuitively rather than rationally to reveal new solutions; but on the negative side, it can warn against emotional instability.

the high priestess

In the Norse card Frigga stands in a pool containing the secrets of the unconscious mind which she alone can divine.

THE EMPRESS

Abundance, fruitfulness and fertility; perhaps marriage or children

The Empress is most often depicted as a mature woman who appears contented and peaceful. The Grand Esoteric, Mythic and Visconti decks all show her in full robes, hinting at pregnancy, a symbol for potential fulfilled: the virgin High Priestess has become a mother. The Norse deck reveals her as a stronger figure, complete with sword and shield. Her number is three, representing the reconciliation of opposites to create a new, third entity. Her path on the Tree of Life is four, linking Hokmah, wisdom, and Binah, understanding.

The Grand Esoteric card shows a ripe corn beside The Empress, standing for a rich and abundant harvest.

El Gran Tarot Esoterico

The Grand Esoteric deck shows a crowned woman in full robes, suggesting a pregnancy, her cloak decorated with leaves, an image of nature's fecundity. She holds a sceptre symbolizing power and a shield engraved with the sun and moon – day and night – representing the union of male and female. At her feet are two lions, symbols of kingship and power, which were worshipped in ancient Egypt. The sun entered the constellation of Leo at about the time of the annual flooding of the Nile. The fertilizing waters refreshed and restored the parched plains, and the population showed their gratitude by worshipping the lion, who had seemingly brought the life-giving water. This could be the origin of the many lion-headed fountains that exist today, where water gushes from the lion's mouth.

The Norse Tarot

The Norse deck uses Freya, an earth goddess, to signify The Empress as a personification of fruitfulness and receptiveness. She is standing in a field of wheat wearing the gold and green colours of an abundant harvest. Freya was the goddess of love and beauty as well as the leader of the Valkyrs, the gods who would choose which dead heroes they would have in their halls. Freya had many followers among women, some of whom would follow their husbands into battle so that they would die with their menfolk, hoping to go with them to Freya's joyful halls. The rune, Ger, ascribed to this card, means harvest, reward for endeavours, fertility and marriage.

The Norse goddess Freya (right) drove a chariot drawn by cats, her sacred animal, and was able to fly in the form of a falcon, as indicated by her winged headdress.

THE EMPRESS

The Mythic Tarot

The Mythic Tarot uses the Greek goddess Demeter to depict The Empress. She stands in a field of ripening corn, her dress woven out of the fruits and flowers of the fertile earth. In the distance water falls into a pool to symbolize the union of male and female, which combines to produce new life. She wears a twelve-stoned necklace that stands for the twelve months of the year, the twelve signs of the zodiac, and the twelve hours of day and night. She represents the natural cycles of nature: of birth, blossom, fruit and decay. Demeter was inconsolable when her beloved daughter, Persephone, was kidnapped by Hades, lord of the underworld. She refused to attend her duties as mother of the harvest, so the crops died and fruits withered on the trees until a bargain was struck with Hades to return Persephone to her mother's land for nine months of the year. During the three months each year when she was without her daughter, Demeter mourned and grieved; the world grew barren and dark, and no crops nor fruits would grow. But, when Persephone was due to return, Demeter would deck the world with the bright flowers of spring to welcome her back.

| STUDENT | *It sounds as though The Empress stands for sorrow as well as fertility and delight.* |

| JULIET | That is right. Demeter symbolizes both sides of motherhood, the joyful side that gives birth and nurtures the young, as well as the |
mournful mother who must face the inevitable separation from her children. The Empress is mother to all sorts of creations, not just physical children; but allowing any creation a life of its own can be a bitter-sweet experience.

The Mythic card images The Empress crowned with a diadem of cities, castles and villages to signify her rulership over homes.

The Cary-Yale Visconti Tarocchi

The Visconti deck shows an imposing-looking woman whose high-waisted, flowing robes indicate a possible pregnancy. She is attended by two hand-maidens, and at her feet stand two children who may be symbols of fertility and new life. She appears powerful and productive, rich and regal, as though her ambitions are satisfied. She is crowned with gold and carries a thin sceptre in her right hand. The imperial eagle of the Holy Roman Empire is emblazoned on her shield, a symbol which was used by the Visconti family after they were officially declared leaders of Milan by the Roman emperor.

Interpreting THE EMPRESS

This card is a symbol of potential fulfilled and is an image for love, marriage or motherhood. It may mean the birth of a either a physical or a creative 'child', for both need patient and careful nurturing. The Empress reflects domestic stability, protection and maternal care. She can indicate a time of security and the establishment of a sound footing for future growth. The card represents peace and comfort or, in its negative form, stagnation and suffocation.

The Visconti card shows a shield decorated with an eagle which is a symbol of the soul enthroned in nature.

THE EMPEROR

Material success, stability, authority and ambition

The Emperor in most decks is portrayed as a richly robed man, generally seated on a throne holding an orb and sceptre to indicate his power and authority. The Emperors in the Russian, Morgan-Greer and Visconti decks all show him in this way, wearing a crown and looking authoritative, while the Ukiyoe deck depicts him looking equally forceful in formal costume. His number is four, which symbolizes solidity, form and concrete organization. His path is five on the Tree of Life, linking Tifereth, meaning beauty, with Hokmah, meaning wisdom.

IV — THE EMPEROR

In the Morgan-Greer card The Emperor holds a sword which symbolizes masculine potency and creativity.

The Morgan-Greer Tarot

The Emperor of the Morgan-Greer deck is shown seated on a throne in the open air. Unlike the landscape in which The Empress is found, his surroundings are stark and infertile. This reflects the barrenness of a masculine world when founded solely on the power of the mind, excluding the softer feminine attributes represented in The Empress. He wears a golden-eagle crown which may link him to the Greek god Zeus, known as the All Father. The eagle appears again on his throne and is also a symbol of the spirit which may be purified through self-control and will-power. The Emperor wears a rich cloak with a golden clasp over his armour, suggesting that his material wealth may conceal his inner strength and might. He is portrayed in this deck in profile to indicate the exterior aspect of his power whose other side is obscured. The Emperor is the Great Father and his wisdom is of an earthly nature; his skill is in handling the material side of life, and his energy is channelled towards turning creative ideas into something solid and workable. While The Empress's energy is nurturing and receptive, The Emperor's is dynamic and outgoing. Together, The Emperor and Empress form a pair.

STUDENT *Does The Emperor have an association with other mythological figures?*

JULIET Yes, as a father archetype, The Emperor can be associated with several father gods. For instance, one link is with the magically resurrected Egyptian king Osiris, father of Horus, who avenged his father's death and became king in his place. After death, Egyptian rulers were believed to become the underworld god Osiris. The Emperor can also be connected with the Greek god Zeus, who established a new order of rule and a hierarchy of gods who obeyed the laws he dictated. Although sometimes autocratic, he was also capable of compassion and care.

The Cary-Yale Visconti Tarocchi

In the Visconti deck, The Emperor is seated on a golden throne and wearing a large, plumed hat, the black imperial eagle embroidered on the brim. His image is powerful, successful and he gives an air of one whose ambitions have been gratified. Four young servants attend him, one kneeling with a golden crown in his hands. The page on the lower left of the image may have had the Visconti family motto, 'A bon droyt' meaning 'To the good belong the right', inscribed on the front of his tunic. The image is one of worldly possessions, power and authority.

The Russian Tarot of St Petersburg

The Russian deck depicts The Emperor in traditional style, seated on his throne of office which is carved with the image of Saint George, the patron saint of chivalry, engaged in his fabled fight with a dragon, symbolizing strength and courage. The Emperor's jewelled robes and gem-encrusted crown represent his status and material wealth. He acts as a link between the ideal and the real, bridging the gap and producing something tangible out of the abyss which lies between those worlds. His role is to create order out of chaos, like the benevolent yet firm father who trains and teaches his child to be an autonomous individual. He is the obvious partner of The Empress and, if The Empress represents the female side of nature, then The Emperor represents the male side.

The domes shown in the distance behind The Emperor in the Russian card (left) are most characteristic of the country.

The Emperor in the Visconti card has his hand on a golden orb which stands for rational thought and understanding of the natural world.

The Ukiyoe Tarot

Here The Emperor is depicted in ceremonial costume, ready to receive his audience. According to an eighth-century chronicle, the Japanese Emperor had divine authority. The Shinto sun goddess proclaimed to her grandson that he and his descendants were to rule Japan, where the Emperor held the seat of religious power as well as being the keeper of Japanese culture. His power may not be as obviously worldly as the other Emperors but he still conveys an impression of dignified authority.

Interpreting THE EMPEROR

The Emperor suggests a time in which matters pertaining to the material world will be important. There is a need to confront personal responsibility because this card emphasizes the necessity of translating dreams into actuality. Matters relating to worldly gain, status or achievement are likely to be important. It could signify an opportunity to start a business or establish a home. The Emperor may represent an influential authority figure, perhaps a father figure. At either end of the spectrum he may prove to be a powerful friend or an unbending tyrant.

The Ukiyoe card shows The Emperor established in his palace and ruling his kingdom with serenity.

THE HIEROPHANT

Guidance on religious matters and the need to find spiritual meaning in life

The Hierophant, or Pope, traditionally appears in papal robes. In the Marseilles and Grand Esoteric deck he is depicted quite formally as a priest or pope, while the Norse deck shows him on a wagon and the Mythic Tarot breaks with tradition completely to picture him as a Centaur. What the four decks have in common though is that he always appears between two pillars, symbolizing his role in the balancing of opposites. His number is five, which indicates mental inspiration, intellectual synthesis, and the four cardinal points united in a common core. His path on the Tree of Life is six, linking Hokmah, wisdom, and Hesed, meaning love and kindness.

The Hierophant's golden triple-tiered crown in the Marseilles card represents his wisdom in the physical, emotional and mental spheres of human existence.

Le Tarot de Marseilles

Here we see a pope-like figure, robed and crowned. The triple-barred papal cross in his left hand can be interpreted as an emblem of the Trinity and demonstrates his spiritual authority. Before him kneel two figures, seemingly receiving his blessing. They may represent all duality in life, such as male and female, thought and desire, good and evil, or life and death. The Hierophant has been linked with Zeus as the supreme god in whose hands lay the power to absolve a man of his sins. Zeus was approached for absolution through his priests and this notion passed into Christianity, with the pope and his bishops becoming the dispensers of divine blessing. The old word for priest was pontifex, meaning 'maker of bridges', and establishes the role of the priest as making a link between man and God. Similarly, The Hierophant represents a spiritual guide within each of us that seeks to establish an inner line of communication between everyday consciousness and an intuitive understanding of spiritual law. With his right hand The Hierophant makes the Christian sign of blessing, called the 'sign of esotericism', with the thumb and first two fingers outstretched (representing the Holy Trinity) and the remaining fingers folded onto the palm (representing male and female).

> **STUDENT** *You have mentioned that The Emperor and The Empress made a pair. Is the same true of The Hierophant and The High Priestess?*

> **JULIET** Yes, The Emperor and The Empress form an earthly pair, representing the qualities of masculine and feminine in the material world, while The Hierophant and The High Priestess represent the same in the spiritual world. The feminine world of The High Priestess is impenetrable by the intellect – an elusive world which cannot be understood by the mind alone – while The Hierophant is the spiritual guide whose teachings are more direct; hence his name, which means 'the revealer of sacred things'.

El Gran Tarot Esoterico

The Grand Esoteric Tarot depicts The Hierophant bareheaded, wearing the triple-tiered cross on his breast as his only ornament. His hand forms the sign of blessing, and a similar symbol appears out of a cloud above him, pointing down to The Hierophant who, in turn, points to mankind. This symbolizes the distinction between 'above' and 'below', between God and man, and identifies The Hierophant as bridge-builder between the two. The pillars behind, one black, the other red, represent obedience and disobedience, law and liberty: the choices which confronted Adam and Eve in Eden.

The Norse Tarot

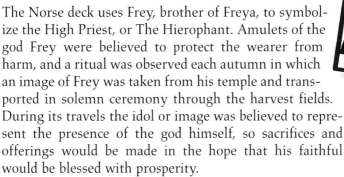

The Norse deck uses Frey, brother of Freya, to symbolize the High Priest, or The Hierophant. Amulets of the god Frey were believed to protect the wearer from harm, and a ritual was observed each autumn in which an image of Frey was taken from his temple and transported in solemn ceremony through the harvest fields. During its travels the idol or image was believed to represent the presence of the god himself, so sacrifices and offerings would be made in the hope that his faithful would be blessed with prosperity.

The Norse card (left) shows Frey being carried by his attendants on his ceremonial passage through the harvest fields.

In the Esoteric card one pillar bears a pentacle to signify earth, while the other carries the emblem of spiritual wings.

The Mythic Tarot

The Mythic deck departs from traditional imagery by portraying Chiron, the Centaur, who was tutor to many young Greek princes, instilling in them spiritual values and respect for divine law. He was a spiritual guide without representing a particular religious path. A strange creature, half-horse, half-man, he was gravely wounded but could not die because of his divine parentage. His suffering gave him a deep understanding of human pain and opened him to genuine compassion, just as a true priest is open to the world's pain because he himself suffers like the martyrs of old. The spiritual law Chiron imparts is personal rather than collective, and signifies the unique relationship each of us must forge with our own particular idea of God.

THE HIEROPHANT

Interpreting THE HIEROPHANT

This card suggests that it is time for the seeker to turn his or her attention towards spiritual matters. It signifies a desire for true understanding of a philosophical or spiritual nature and a wish to find real purpose or meaning in life. This may arise in the search for a guide or spiritual mentor, perhaps in the form of a priest or psychotherapist, or a study of a religious or philosophical nature. On a positive level, it indicates that freedom may be acquired through knowledge, and negatively, that bad advice is given or power is misused by withholding information.

Chiron holds a scroll of wisdom identifying him as a teacher. With his other hand he makes an ancient sign of blessing, older than the sign used in the other decks.

THE LOVERS

A relationship or love affair with a trial or choice involved

The Lovers card most commonly portrays a young man seemingly caught undecided between two women. The Ukiyoe and the Marseilles decks follow this theme, while the Visconti deck shows a couple pledging their troth with a blindfolded cupid above. The Rider-Waite Tarot departs from tradition by using Adam and Eve as the pair of lovers faced with a choice. The number of this card is six, which is a number of harmony, and its path on the Tree of Life is seven, linking Tifereth, beauty, with Binah meaning intelligence or understanding.

In the Marseilles card the choice is between an older woman with dark hair and a younger, blonde girl. Cupid points his arrow towards youth and beauty.

Le Tarot de Marseilles

This deck depicts a young man apparently torn between two women, while a winged cupid hovers above. The Lovers card is thought by many writers to have used the myth of the Judgement of Paris as its inspiration. Paris, a mortal, was called upon to judge a beauty competition between three goddesses, Hera, wife of Zeus and queen of heaven, the warrior Athene, and Aphrodite, goddess of love and beauty. All three had caught a golden apple addressed 'To the Fairest' and each thought herself to be more worthy of the title; so Zeus summoned Paris to settle the dispute. Each goddess resorted to bribery: Hera with wealth and power, Athena offering victory in battle, while Aphrodite simply offered him the hand of the most beautiful woman in the world. And, just for good measure, Eros, Aphrodite's son, fired a gold-tipped arrow at Paris, who then awarded Aphrodite the golden apple without further ado. Aphrodite kept her promise and gave him the hand of the beautiful Helen of Sparta, who was, inconveniently, already married to someone else. When Paris claimed his prize, the Trojan War was started.

STUDENT | *It sounds as though this myth is a warning of the dangers involved in letting your passions run away with you!*

JULIET | Yes, it does point out the far-reaching consequences of a hasty or rash choice in love. Some decks show a striking difference between the women: one is young and beautiful, the other older and less attractive. This seems to suggest the young man is poised between a mother and a sweetheart, his love for his mother and his desire for sexual liaisons, his conscience and his passions, or even between security and independence. Of course the choice that this card implies will not always be to do with love or romance, but it is likely that it will be a matter of great personal importance. The Lovers also involves loss because to choose one thing means to give up another.

The Cary-Yale Visconti Tarocchi

This deck shows two young people facing each other and clasping hands. Their faces look open and happy, as though they are eager for a relationship. Above them hovers a blindfolded Cupid holding up his arrows, ready to fall without election or purpose. The Greek version of Cupid was Eros, son of Chaos, a primal urge and life force. He degenerated in Roman art to the chubby mischievous winged child who tormented and tricked humans with his arrows of desire. Either way – blind and unconsidered or as a nasty trick of the gods – love can be both a blessing and a curse.

The Rider-Waite Tarot

This deck uses Adam and Eve to illustrate the theme of choice. The image is of a man and woman standing in the Garden of Eden. Adam stands before the Tree of Life which bears twelve fruit, one for each sign of the zodiac. Eve stands in front the Tree of Knowledge, from which fruits hang, representing the five senses. Adam and Eve were tempted and ate of the forbidden fruit, choosing sex and reproduction which made them godlike in the creation of new life. However, as well as bringing the gift of producing life, their choice also brought death, albeit with the possibility of spiritual immortality.

Cupid is sometimes shown blindfolded, as here in the Visconti card, to symbolize the blindness of love and the indiscriminate way the gods wound or favour with love.

Around the trunk of the Tree of Knowledge the Rider-Waite card (above left) shows a coiled serpent, an ancient symbol of wisdom and sex.

The Ukiyoe Tarot

In this deck a young man is depicted walking with a courtesan, a prostitute carefully trained in erotic arts. The young woman is brightly dressed in pastel colours, suggesting sensuality and the promise of romance, while on the young man's left stands an older woman, soberly dressed in grays and blacks, representing convention and suitable status. According to old Japanese tradition, marriages were pre-arranged for adolescent boys and girls, so the young men often looked for romance with courtesans in the pleasure quarters of the cities. The young man is apparently faced with a difficult choice between sensual gratification and the path of virtue and merit.

Interpreting THE LOVERS

This card represents a situation or relationship which is of great personal importance to the seeker and which will involve choices, although not necessarily in the area of love. Choices inevitably involve a degree of disappointment because if something is chosen, something else must be relinquished. Adam and Eve chose knowledge, but along with that came death. To choose love and passion can also bring pain and hurt. The particular circumstance will have to be fully discussed with the seeker to understand the context of his or her situation.

The Ukiyoe card shows a nymph of beauty carrying a pink flower, a symbol of attraction and love.

THE CHARIOT

A struggle or conflict, yet strong potential for triumph over adversity

The image in The Chariot card is most commonly one of a man driving a chariot drawn by two differently coloured horses pulling in opposite directions. The Rider-Waite deck moves away from the traditional horses to depict two sphinxes drawing the chariot, while the Norse deck figures goats; yet the struggle to control conflicting forces and urges remains universal to this card. Its number is seven, the number of progress, self-expression and triumph, and its path on the Tree of Life is eight, linking Binah, intelligence, and Geburah, meaning power and strength.

The four pillars, the canopy and the two sphinxes in the Rider-Waite card add up to seven, the number which governs the underlying rhythms of the universe.

The Rider-Waite Tarot

This deck shows The Chariot as an armour-clad figure standing in a battle vehicle. A star-studded canopy represents the heavens, while the chariot stands for the earth, together announcing the dictum 'as above, so below'. The four pillars represent the four conditions in which energy can survive, namely fire, air, water and earth, or electricity, gas, liquid and solid. The chariot is drawn by two sphinxes, one black, the other white, symbolizing the riddle which the charioteer must solve. On his shoulders lie two crescent moons to reflect his mastery over fluctuating emotions, which are lunar and feminine, while his golden armour reflects his forceful outgoing energy, which is solar and masculine. The crescent moons are also connected with the number seven, as the moon completes each phase of her cycle in seven days. The charioteer must steer a steady middle path between his opposing thoughts and feelings. The Chariot is an image of the constant interplay involved in balancing opposites – masculine and feminine, strength and weakness, positive and negative – with the upright charioteer appearing as the point of equilibrium. Thus the essence of this card is the reconciliation of the conflicts caused by opposing forces.

STUDENT — *So are you saying that the chariot and its driver represent our conscious mind while the horses stand for the different impulses we have to cope with?*

JULIET — That's right. Plato speaks of the lover's soul as a charioteer driving two winged horses, 'the noble steed of reason' and 'the ignoble one of passionate desire'. That may sound a little outdated today, but the horses can represent conflict in the form of *knowing* you should do one thing, yet *wanting* to do another. We are constantly having to weigh and balance our desires with our rational minds. Trying, like the charioteer, to drive an even course between the two extremes.

The Norse Tarot

The Norse Tarot uses Thor, the god of thunder and lightning, to illustrate The Chariot. He is depicted in a chariot drawn by two goats, Tanngniortr (toothgrinder) and Tanngrisnr (toothgnasher). Thunder was explained as being the rumbling wheels of Thor's chariot crossing the sky, while flashes of lightning were said to be sparks of anger flying from his long red beard. Despite all this ferocity, Thor was considered a generous god, a sort of 'gentle giant', kind and calm until provoked, when he would break out into tempestuous rages.

The Mythic Tarot

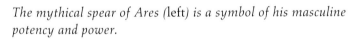

THE CHARIOT

This deck depicts the Greek god of war, Ares, whose love of conflict and struggle made him unpopular with many of the Olympian gods. They prized above all else refinement, beauty and civilized behaviour, and so considered him unnecessarily coarse and aggressive. Nevertheless, Aphrodite loved him for his ardour and passion. The affair between the goddess of Love and the god of War produced a child whose name was Harmony. Here the charioteer is pictured keeping a tight grip on the two powerful steeds that clearly wish to go in different directions. The energy with which he reins in the animals suggests he has a good chance of mastering them.

The Norse god Thor carries his symbol, a magic hammer which would always return to his hand like a boomerang.

The mythical spear of Ares (left) is a symbol of his masculine potency and power.

The 1JJ Swiss Tarot

Once again we see an armoured man holding a staff; yet he is disconnected from his chariot which is drawn by horses without reins. The Chariot has been connected with the myth of Phaeton, son of Helios the sun god, whose chariot bearing the sun would light the day. One day, the inexperienced Phaeton got up earlier than his father and took the sun chariot out alone. He soon learned that he could not control the powerful horses as skilfully as his father, and the chariot plunged wildly towards earth, alternately scorching or freezing everything below, as the sun drew first too near and then too far away. Zeus was obliged to send a thunderbolt to destroy Phaeton before the foolhardy son destroyed the earth.

Interpreting THE CHARIOT

This card suggests struggle and conflict ahead; yet there is also a chance for resolution of such difficulties. It shows there is plenty of the energy and drive required to achieve goals. On a positive note it indicates the determination and self-assertion that is necessary for success. Its more negative associations are those of aggression and forcefulness without due consideration for others.

The horses symbolize libido, and so suggest that the charioteer needs to gain mastery over his instincts.

JUSTICE

Balance, wisdom and a need for rational, logical solutions

The traditional image for Justice is of a figure holding a pair of scales and a sword. The Rider-Waite and the Witches decks follow this picture, while the Haindl deck is more abstract. The Grand Esoteric Tarot departs from the tradition by recalling the legend of Solomon. There is some disagreement about the order of the trumps and the sequence has been 'rectified' so often that it is impossible to know the original one. Older decks give Justice eleven and Strength eight. On the Tree of Life its path is twelve, connecting Geburah, power and strength, with Tifereth, beauty.

The Rider-Waite Tarot

The Rider-Waite deck shows Justice as a throned figure, crowned with gold and holding an upright sword and evenly balanced scales. She is seated between two pillars which depict the eternal opposites, with a purple veil, the colour of wisdom, connecting them. Justice wears a green cloak which is the colour of Venus and of love, over a red robe, the colour of Mars and of war; so her dress combines to symbolize balance between opposing forces. Athene, the wise goddess of the Greeks, is sometimes linked with the Justice card for, although a warrior, she used the power of the mind and the intellect to its fullest extent both in battles and as a judge of difficult situations. Her preference in war was to use guile and diplomacy rather than brute force to win her battles. She would always use logic over bloodthirsty combat.

The Tarot of the Witches

The Witches deck shows Justice wearing a blindfold; yet her eyes are visible beneath it to suggest that justice is deliberately dispensed, not randomly. Again, we see the balanced scales, and she is holding a double-edged sword, indicating that she can perceive and penetrate through to the heart of all situations, and a faint red heart on her left cheek symbolizes her virtue and goodness. The snake which she is trampling denotes injustice, and may represent humankind and human nature. Behind Justice in the background, a glowing scarlet sky suggests the rising sun, mirroring the power of her moral strength and integrity.

The scales in the Rider-Waite card are feminine and the sword masculine, echoing the theme of balance and equality.

In the Witches card (right) Justice wears her hair in neat, even strands, indicating moderation and equality.

JUSTICE

El Gran Tarot Esoterico

The image on this deck probably describes the story of Solomon, King of Israel, who was credited with transcendent wisdom. According to the Old Testament, when Solomon came to the throne he was told by God to name any wish his heart desired. The young king immediately asked for an understanding heart so that he might judge his people and discover the difference between good and bad. The Lord was pleased with his choice and granted him such wisdom and understanding that neither before nor since has anyone been as wise as Solomon. On one occasion, the great king was asked to judge over a dispute between two women, one of whose baby had died, and who both laid claim to the same living baby which they carried between them. Solomon suggested he take his sword and cut the baby in half which caused the real mother to offer her child to her enemy rather than see it die; and so Solomon was able to make his wise judgement.

> **STUDENT** *Solomon's decision to cut the baby in half appears to be a very cold one. Is that reflected in the Justice card?*

> **JULIET** Yes, but only in that Justice reflects fairness and impartiality, and not necessarily warmth and compassion. Justice raises us above nature and stands for absolute equality. However, equality can be cold and unfeeling, so Justice needs to be tempered with mercy, which is, after all, what Solomon eventually dispensed.

The Grand Esoteric card shows a crowned king raising his sword as though to halve the naked baby.

The Haindl Tarot

The Haindl deck shows scales of balance, one silver, reflecting the feminine, and one gold for the masculine. They hang from an invisible holder, perhaps suggesting that justice exists in the universe as a perfect principle yet it is not of this world. The Justice card is often linked with the Egyptian concept of judgement after death, when a soul was weighed in a set of scales against the feather of the goddess Maat, the principle of order and truth. The dead person's conscience had to weigh exactly the same as the feather in order to pass the test which would free him forever from mortal misery. The feathers in this image seem precarious in that they could easily have their order disrupted by a simple breath of wind. They are attached to the trunk of a tree which is a reminder that the spiritual and the natural world do not exist in isolation from each other. The 'eyes' in the peacock feathers indicate the need to see and understand emotions.

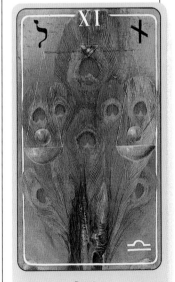

Justice

Interpreting JUSTICE

Justice represents the need to weigh things carefully and rationally in order to find fair, dispassionate solutions to current problems. It suggests there may be occasion for arbitration or that agreements may be reached through negotiation. Possibly the seeker is involved in legal dealings and there is a need for balanced thought and impartial decision making. Its negative interpretation might be injustice or a lack of fair dealing.

The cosmic balls in the Haindl card are suspended from above to symbolize equilibrium.

THE HERMIT

A time for soul searching and meditation; a need for patience and solitude

The Hermit is most commonly depicted in the traditional decks as an old, bearded man, simply dressed and carrying a staff and lantern. The decks figured below conform to this image, with the exception of the Visconti deck, whose Hermit carries an hour-glass instead of a lantern. The number of The Hermit is nine, the number of initiation and the last of the single numbers out of which all higher numbers are composed. The Hermit's path on the Tree of Life is ten, linking Hesed, kindness, with Tifereth, meaning beauty.

The Hermit in the Russian deck is dressed in a hooded cloak and has a long grey beard which symbolizes age and experience.

The Russian Tarot of St Petersburg

The Russian Tarot depicts The Hermit looking to the left of the picture as though reflecting on his past. Behind him lie barren mountains, and the night sky studded with stars mirrors the dark night of the soul. The old man trudges on with only his lantern for comfort and his staff for support. There are echoes of The Fool in this card for, like him, The Hermit is depicted as a traveller, alone, with little to give him direction. The big difference between them is that the image of The Fool is carefree and confident, like the child or youth with everything before him. The Hermit is The Fool grown older and wiser, and having learned through experience he is now cautious. He has acquired the precious boon of patience and wisdom which can only be attained through the passage of time. The Hermit has learned to be alone which means he does not have to depend on others; he can rely on himself.

The 1JJ Swiss Tarot

In this deck The Hermit is shown as a monk with shaven head and coarse brown robes. He appears to be treading the path of the pilgrim, solitary and withdrawn. The pilgrim is an inspiration to others as his light shines not only for himself but for the world. This figure has been identified by a number of authors as possessing the cardinal virtue of Prudence. The Hermit has been likened to Saint Jude, the patron saint of hopeless cases, whose help is invoked in desperate situations or when all else has failed. Although a solitary figure, The Hermit is not unhappy.

The lantern carried by The Hermit (right) symbolizes reason and knowledge, the light of higher consciousness.

The Cary-Yale Visconti Tarocchi

Here The Hermit is wearing rich red robes with gold embellishment, and an unusual two-tiered hat. In one hand he holds a staff, and in the other a large hourglass which is a symbol of the ever-running sands of time. The Hermit has been connected with the Jungian archetype of the Wise Old Man, a teacher who can offer deep insights and invaluable guidance. He has also been linked with the Greek god Cronus, whose name means time. Cronus created and ruled over the Golden Age, which was a time of plenty. As the god of time, he established the cycles of nature and the timing of birth, blossom, fruit and decay. However, he could not accept the laws that he himself had created; so when an oracle proclaimed that he would be overthrown by his son, he proceeded to swallow his children at birth. Eventually the oracle proved correct and Zeus dethroned Cronus after a long struggle. This myth describes the fear we all feel about old age and death; yet the dethroned Cronus eventually found another role for himself as the god of old age, as well as time, and, according to legend, is waiting for the dawning of a new Golden Age.

The Hermit's heavy cloak in the Visconti card stands for the protection acquired through self-knowledge and possession.

The Haindl Tarot

The Haindl deck retains the basic image of an old man with a lighted lamp, symbolizing human knowledge and teachings which are passed down through generations. The Hermit's stick or staff has been described in many different ways by as many different writers. One is as a phallic staff, which suggests his deep knowledge of the mysterious forces of nature; while another is the staff that condemns wrong doing; and yet another describes the staff as the solace found in faith and belief in God – reminiscent of the biblical quote, 'thy rod and thy staff, they comfort me' (Psalm 23). The cloaked figure here stands on a mountain top surrounded by birds representing the spirit. Strange gnome- and bird-like faces seen emerging from the rocks suggest the elemental spirit forces that are alive in nature. On the bottom right of the image is the astrological glyph for the zodiacal sign Virgo, which shows that, like the virgin, The Hermit is self-sufficient and complete in himself. He may be alone, but he is not lonely. He has found inner peace and wholeness and is content with himself.

The Hermit

Interpreting THE HERMIT

The Hermit describes the passage of time and reveals the wisdom and comfort that can be gained through acceptance. His appearance in a reading suggests the time is ripe for soul-searching, which often requires a period of seclusion, away from the distractions of the busy world. The Hermit can also indicate a wise teacher who can assist in the inner quest for meaning. He represents the wise part within us that can emerge through dreams and visions. The negative aspect of The Hermit might be extreme caution which could result in unnecessary delay, or an inability to let go of old ideas and accept new ones.

By The Hermit's right hand, the Haindl card shows an eye within a triangle, representing the image of God.

THE WHEEL OF FORTUNE

A new chapter is starting; problems are solved through changes in circumstances

The details of imagery in The Wheel of Fortune cards shown here differ considerably but the most consistent theme is one of men, creatures or objects fastened to a turning wheel. The Wheel is number ten, first of the double numbers, thus signifying the completion of one cycle and the beginning of a new one: the first half of the journey in the outer world is complete and the time is approaching for the second, inner, cycle to commence. Its path on the Tree of Life is eleven, linking Hesed, love, and Netsah, meaning endurance.

THE WHEEL OF FORTUNE

The Mythic Tarot

The Mythic Tarot uses the image of the three goddesses of Fate, whom the Greeks called the Moirai. They were the daughters of Night, the oldest power in the universe, and no one, not even Zeus himself, could undo or change their work. However, The Wheel of Fortune does not mean that man's life is preordained in every way. The choices that each man makes about his life are his own. Sometimes we may make foolish choices or unwise decisions and are inclined to blame fate or other people, anything rather than accept responsibility for the outcome of our actions. The Wheel of Fortune card is a curious paradox, standing for both stability and change at once. What Jung called the Self lies hidden deep within the psyche, in much the same way that the hub of the wheel is its least obviously impressive part. It is the rim which moves and attracts attention, yet it is the hub about which the rim turns. It is therefore ultimately responsible for all that comes its way, just as it is our Self, through our actions, which brings us our fate.

The 1JJ Swiss Tarot

This deck shows the goddess Fortuna turning the wheel, so causing fortunes to rise and fall. She is blindfolded, possibly to illustrate that fortune is distributed indiscriminately – 'the rain falls on the just and the unjust alike'. The 1JJ Swiss deck appears to take its imagery from the favourite medieval teachings of the emptiness of worldly aspirations. The lesson was that wealth and material pleasures soon turn to dust and

The Mythic card portrays the Fates weaving the threads of human life in a secret cave: Clotho spun the thread; Lachesis measured its length; and Atropos cut it.

The 1JJ Swiss card (right) shows a rejoicing couple at the top of the wheel celebrating without care, while just below a man falls unnoticed into the abyss.

X

WHEEL of FORTUNE

that humankind's only true hope is in God or the spirit. The Wheel of Fortune represents the steady progression of man to his zenith, the peak of his achievement after which follows defeat and ultimately death. The Wheel is constantly in motion, reminding us that everything passes and nothing lasts so that neither pleasure nor misfortune should be taken too seriously.

WHEEL OF FORTUNE

The Tarot of the Witches

This deck departs from the more traditional images to show The Wheel of Fortune revolving without human help between two dead trees. The Wheel is made from four planks of wood, while nine symbols of fortune surround the rim. Each symbol has its own significance, both pleasant and unpleasant: the star suggests improvement; the shooting comet stands for wealth; the sun symbolizes happiness in love; the rainbow stands for peace after difficulties; and the horseshoe is an image of unexpected pleasure. On the more negative side: the black cloud stands for disaster; the old, bleeding moon signifies misery and disappointment; the dagger is a symbol of deceit; and the broken heart is an unhappy love affair.

The Wheel in the Witches card is about to stop and choose a position while a bird sits on a barren branch, seemingly awaiting the outcome.

The Ukiyoe Tarot

The Ukiyoe deck maintains the symbol of rising, crowning and falling so common to this card. As The Wheel turns, the snake falls and the white fox rises. A traditional way of interpreting this card is to see the animal which is falling, the snake in this deck, as the unevolved soul sinking deep into the traps of the material world. Meanwhile, the white fox shows the soul rising from the snares of the material bonds. The figure holding the sword is waiting to return the soul to The Wheel – after death has finally released it from its human limitations – to endure another incarnation. When the soul has eventually reached the moment of true enlightenment the sword is used to cut the ties with the material world and grant the soul permanent release. The eight-spoked wheel represents the Buddhist Wheel of Doctrine, the eight-fold path to enlightenment. The Eight Noble Paths teach the practice of righteousness in thought, understanding, speech, livelihood, action, effort, mindfulness and concentration, these paths being dedicated to a life of harmony and tranquillity.

THE WHEEL OF FORTUNE

Interpreting THE WHEEL OF FORTUNE

When The Wheel of Fortune appears in a reading, it signifies a new start. A new chapter is opening which is, in itself, neither positive nor negative, yet how the new energies are worked with will determine that. The image of The Wheel, forever turning, can be compared with the turning of the earth on its axis, endlessly revolving, bringing day and night, summer and winter, times of plenty and of shortage. The best way to work with The Wheel is to accept its motion and try to live with what it brings in the most constructive way possible.

The sword in the Ukiyoe card cuts through ignorance and spiritual obstacles in order to find the truth.

STRENGTH

A time for self-awareness involving courage, strength and determination

Strength is shown in some decks as a young woman restraining a lion, a common medieval image as used in the Visconti and Ukiyoe decks. The 1JJ Swiss deck depicts a man engaged in a fierce struggle with a lion, while the Norse deck pictures the binding of a wolf. There has been disagreement about the numbering of Strength: some older decks give Strength eight and Justice eleven, while modern writers, including Waite, give Justice eight and Strength eleven. Its path is nine on the Tree of Life, linking Geburah, power and strength, and Hesed, meaning love and kindness.

The maiden represents the moon and femininity while the lion indicates the sun and masculine energy – jointly they stand for the union of opposites.

The Cary-Yale Visconti Tarocchi

The Visconti deck shows a young woman who is gently but firmly holding open the gaping jaws of a lion. Her face is calm and her expression kind but determined. She has long, golden hair and wears flowing robes which show her to be the personification of feminin-ity; yet she is engaged in a very real struggle with the king of beasts. Greek myth tells the story of Apollo, the sun god, and the lovely Cyrene, who was handmaiden to his sister, the moon god-dess Artemis. Apollo encountered Cyrene while she was in the heat of a fierce struggle with a ferocious lion. He watched the scene, charmed with her fortitude and courage, as well as her delicate beauty; and when Cyrene eventually won her battle, he asked her to live with him in a faraway paradise. This myth suggests that the feminine powers of determination and strength of will can conquer brute force.

The Ukiyoe Tarot

An elegant woman in elaborate dress is holding the lion's jaws open, ren-dering him harmless. The animal is a snow lion, an animal which tradi-tionally guards Japanese shrines. Behind the pair blooms a cherry tree, perhaps symbolizing spring, a time when new life is promised. The image is not a violent one but rather suggests that calm strength can triumph. The woman's mild though authoritative manner persuades the beast to serve human interests rather than put his strength to destructive use.

The Ukiyoe card (right) reveals another image of gentleness winning over the savage beast.

The 1JJ Swiss Tarot

The 1JJ Swiss deck depicts a man struggling with a savage-looking lion; the fight appears to be a serious one. This image recalls the struggle of the Greek hero Herakles with the brutal Nemean lion. The first of Herakles' twelve labours was to destroy this lion, which was both enormous and savage, and had been wantonly depopulating the surrounding area for some time. Herakles fought long and hard, eventually succeeding in destroying the animal. He then flayed the beast's amazingly thick skin, making it into a cloak for himself, using the head as a helmet, thus becoming as powerful as the lion itself. The story hints at the problem of containing the savage beast within ourselves, for the lion is a symbol of forceful instinctual desires which, although they may need to be controlled, also represent the passion and energy of the personality. The fact that Herakles was able to make productive use of the beast's pelt indicates the good that such power can be put to. We, too, need to channel our own desire towards positive creative expression rather than destructive forces.

The Norse Tarot

The Norse deck uses the image of the binding of the wolf Fenris to describe the card Strength. According to Norse myth, Fenris was a monstrous wolf born to the god Loki and the giantess Anguboda. Their other two terrible offspring, the Great Serpent and Hel, goddess of the underworld, were flung into the sea and buried, respectively. But the great god Odin felt sure that, with kindness and understanding, Fenris could be tamed sufficiently to become a servant to the gods. However, to his horror, the wolf increased daily in size and ferocity, and Odin finally came to realize that his wish would not be possible. Having consulted together, the gods decided that killing the wolf would transgress their laws; thus their only course of action would be to secure the beast in such a way that he could do no harm. After a number of abortive attempts, the gods finally obtained a magical rope and challenged the wolf to test his strength against that of the cord. Fenris was suspicious and would only accept the challenge if one of the gods placed his hand between his teeth during the process. Tyr, the courageous god of war, agreed and Fenris was finally bound up for ever. This myth, like the story of Herakles, provides an image of the need to immobilize negative forces.

After failing to kill the lion with clubs and arrows, Herakles eventually strangled the beast with his bare hands, shown here in the Swiss card.

According to Norse mythology, during the struggle with the magic rope, Fenris bit Tyr's hand off at the wrist.

Interpreting STRENGTH

This card indicates the need for courage, strength and determination in order to face the 'lion within'. The lion is a symbol of the potential for great destructiveness as well of royal greatness. Herakles is able to destroy the terrifying aspect of the lion while preserving its wonderful skin for protection. This card offers the possibility for self-awareness and the potential for integration and individuality. Positively, Strength suggests there is an opportunity for reconciliation with the enemy, whether within or without. On a negative level it could suggest a surrender to unworthy impulses or an abuse of power.

THE HANGED MAN

A sacrifice must be made in order to gain something of great value

The most common image for this card is of a man hanging upside down by one foot, yet far from looking tortured, his face is usually calm and serene. The Russian and the Marseilles decks follow this imagery while the Norse and the Mythic decks depart from tradition by depicting the sacrifice of the gods Odin and Prometheus. The Hanged Man's number is twelve, relating to renewal and salvation. His path on the Tree of Life is thirteen, linking Hod, splendour, with Geburah, strength.

The Norse Tarot

The Norse deck depicts the god Odin hanging upside down on the World tree, Yggdrasil, reaching down to find insight and understanding. The tangled roots of the tree can be likened to a puzzle of the unconscious mind, wherein lies a wisdom which is not easily obtained. Odin hanged himself on the tree voluntarily for nine days and nights, without food or water, wounding himself with his own spear – 'myself consecrated to myself'. His agony was intense, yet he endured this torture in order to gain secret knowledge and power. Eventually, Odin was rewarded with the discovery of the sacred runes. Other stories of Odin tell that he sacrificed one of his eyes in order to obtain inner sight; again we have the idea of giving something up in order to gain something even more important.

The Mythic Tarot

The Mythic deck uses Prometheus as The Hanged Man to represent an image of sacrifice. According to Greek myth, Prometheus was the Titan who created mankind and, loving his creations dearly, wanted them to be more godlike. He therefore stole divine fire from Olympus to give to man, for which he was cruelly punished by Zeus: chained to icy rocks high in the mountains, Zeus' eagle ate out his liver by day, only for it grow back each night in time for the torture to be repeated. Prometheus stole the fire in the full knowledge of what this act would mean in terms of punishment; yet he loved mankind so much that he was prepared to make the sacrifice.

The Norse card portrays Odin's spear on which he carved the sacred runes through which he gained wisdom, strength and mastery.

Men and women wore rings in commemoration of the bondage of Prometheus, their creator and benefactor, shown here in the Mythic card (right).

THE HANGED MAN

The Russian Tarot of St Petersburg

The Russian Tarot shows The Hanged Man in traditional Slavic costume hanging from a tree. This may link The Hanged Man with the common theme of the dying and rising god, whose yearly death and resurrection was believed to guarantee the annual rebirth of the crops; this in turn suggests the promise of life after death. The tree from which he is hanging is heavy with apples, reminiscent of some medieval paintings of Christ crucified on a fruit-laden tree. This imagery is demonstrating that death is not final, there is always an opportunity for resurrection and rebirth. The shape of the figure – an inverted triangle beneath the cross of the tree – symbolizes the descent of higher into lower, the conscious into the unconscious.

| STUDENT | *Does the image of The Hanged Man originate from Christ's crucifixion?* |

| JULIET | The image of a hanging man is possibly pre-Christian and |
may derive from hanging straw dolls in the fields to denote the dying and rising god of the crop. Some writers, however, have connected this card with the sacrifice of Jesus dying on the cross to give humankind eternal life. Some old decks depict The Hanged Man with money falling out of his pockets, perhaps a reference to Judas, who betrayed Jesus for thirty pieces of silver and then hanged himself. It could also refer to a desire to discard material wealth in favour of spiritual richness, which fits in with the general meaning of sacrifice connected with this card.

The Russian card shows the fairy-tale firebird eating the apples that grow around The Hanged Man.

Le Tarot de Marseilles

The Marseilles deck, like the Russian deck, shows a man hanging from a tree with one leg tucked behind the other, his arms tied behind his back. This suggests that the traditional values of society are turned upside down: the truth is the opposite of that which it appears to be. The fact that The Hanged Man is suspended by his foot may indicate a link with Pisces, the zodiacal sign which rules the feet. Pisces is often connected with sacrifice, dissolution and death as it is the last sign of the zodiac. It corresponds with the final stages of winter, dying slowly before the birth of spring. The time of year during which the sun passes through Pisces also corresponds to Lent, which, for Christians, is a time of self-sacrifice and spiritual cleansing, recalling the sufferings endured by Christ prior to his crucifixion and subsequent resurrection.

Although his posture looks most uncomfortable, the expression on the man's face in the Marseilles card is peaceful; he seems serene and composed.

Interpreting THE HANGED MAN

There is a need for sacrifice. This will involve giving something up in order to get something of greater value or significance. It is important to remember the voluntary aspect of this card: that there are choices to be taken and judgements to be made about what is important and what can be dispensed with. The notion of exchanging the mundane for the spiritual is the central theme of The Hanged Man.

DEATH

Changes: the end of the old and the birth of the new

Most versions of this card depict Death as a skeleton, sometimes riding a horse and sometimes cutting down life with his scythe, as in the Visconti deck. The Grand Esoteric Tarot portrays a skeleton riding a cat, while the Morgan-Greer and Haindl decks both show a river in the background. They all feature the scythe as a symbol of the Grim Reaper. His number is thirteen which symbolizes order – Death, although apparently destructive, actually brings a new order. On the Tree of Life his path is fourteen, linking Netsah, endurance, and Tifereth, beauty.

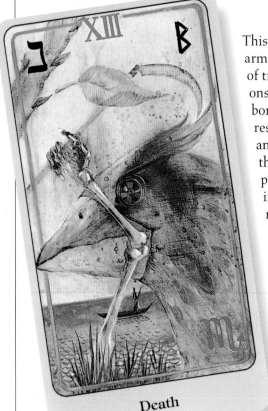

Death

The Haindl card bears the astrological glyph of Scorpio, associated in astrological tradition with transformation, death and rebirth.

The Haindl Tarot

This deck shows a scythe, a traditional image for Death, held in the arm of a skeleton. The skeleton is not a symbol of death, but rather of transformation, for it is the part of the body most resistant to the onslaught of time – the flesh rots but the bone remains. These bones also symbolize the mineral world; the grass and the tree represent the plant world; the bird stands for the animal kingdom; and the figure in the boat represents the world of humans. All these worlds transform through the continuous cycle of growth: plants grow, are eaten by the animal or human world, whose inhabitants die and decompose, in due course providing life to new growth.

The Hebrew letter ascribed to this card is *nun* which means fish. The fish was an early Christian symbol of Christ as the redeemer who conquers death and, through death, achieves everlasting life for all. The boat in the background alludes to the mythical Greek boatman, Charon, who would ferry the souls of the dead across the river Styx to the entrance of Hades. However, the boat was originally a symbol of a baby's cradle, standing for birth as well as death.

STUDENT *I have always been afraid of Death in the tarot thinking it meant physical death.*

JULIET Death in the tarot refers to endings, to changes, and to cycles which are over. The card can just as easily refer to the death of single life which occurs with marriage, to the death of school days when they end, or to the end of life lived in one place when you move to another. These are changes, transition phases even, which we view as positive and therefore do not normally associate with Death, a card we tend to see as negative. But any ending is like a little death whether it comes in the form of marriage or divorce. Endings inevitably involve some sadness; there is often a time of nostalgia, when the time comes to move on, and a period of mourning needs to be acknowledged.

Cary-Yale Visconti Tarocchi

The skeleton of Death in this deck rides roughshod over a huddle of people, sweeping his scythe to cut them down as he passes. The group includes a pope and a cardinal as well as ordinary folk, revealing Death as the great leveller: for everyone turns to dust in their grave no matter how rich, powerful, strong or even holy they have been in their lives. Endings are an inevitable part of life and cannot be avoided – even the mighty must one day fall.

The Morgan-Greer Tarot

Death in the Morgan-Greer deck shows a skeleton cloaked in black with a white rose in front of him. Black is the colour of death, while white symbolizes purity; so together they signify the purification of the mind, body

and spirit through death, in preparation for rebirth. The river may represent the Greek Styx, or the river Jordan which Christian souls must cross in order to gain entry to heaven. The Greek dead had to be buried with a coin on their tongue as payment to Hades for entrance to his kingdom. Without this money the soul could not enter his land; nor could it return to life, so it would be a ghost trapped between two worlds. The coin represents the period of mourning we must go through whenever anything changes or ends before we can fully enter into the new phase of life.

The skeleton's headdress in the Visconti card is made up from the shreds of a shroud.

The flow of the river towards the sea in the Morgan-Greer card (left) symbolizes the flow of life towards death.

El Gran Tarot Esoterico

Death appears here riding a cat. He tramples over the crowns of royalty and the clergy, symbols of power and authority; the head of a young woman, signifying beauty; as well as swords and weapons which suggest that there is no fight Death cannot win when his moment comes. The tomb in the background has an ankh, the Egyptian symbol for life, on the door. And the plants sprouting in the foreground suggest that new life and death lie side by side. Death in this image is lively compared with the forbidding figure of the other decks. It seems to represent a liberator whose sharp scythe cuts through old bonds to release new life and spirit. The inside of his cloak is red, the colour of Mars, the fiery planet of hot passion ruling Scorpio, the sign of transformation.

Interpreting DEATH

In a reading, Death signifies that something is drawing to its natural close. It depends largely on how the seeker feels about the particular matter as to how painful or not that ending will be. The Death card automatically suggests new life, but endings and new beginnings are both exciting and frightening. Death is necessary, it is part of the cycle of life – it is best to work with it rather than against it.

In the Esoteric deck, Death's black cloak is decorated with stars and moons, perhaps suggesting that death is as old and mysterious as they are.

TEMPERANCE

Mixing and blending of opposites; compromise and cooperation

The traditional portrayal of Temperance is a woman carefully pouring liquid from one cup to another. This is an image of moderation and is followed by all four cards shown below. Temperance is usually assigned the number fourteen: its component figures, one and four, combine to make five, a number symbolizing growth, inspiration and the reconciliation of many parts to a greater whole. The path of Temperance on the Tree of Life is fifteen, connecting Tifereth, beauty, and Yesod, foundation.

The Mythic Tarot

The winged woman in the Mythic Tarot represents Iris, the Greek messenger goddess of the rainbow; and just as a rainbow links heaven and earth, so Iris acted as a link between the gods and humankind. She is depicted here encircled by a rainbow, a symbol of hope and promise – the sign made by God to Noah after the Great Flood to promise that he would never destroy the earth with water again; so when a rainbow appears in the sunlight during a shower, it brings a feeling of optimism.

The Temperance angel is shown, in accordance with tradition, pouring liquid from a gold cup, signifying masculine, solar, conscious energy, into a silver one, representing feminine, lunar, unconscious energy – the two energies joined together by the flow of feeling. She stands with one foot in the water and the other on land, which echoes the notion of bridging the gap between the inner and outer, the unconscious and the conscious mind. The flow of liquid between the cups indicates the constant movement necessary in order to preserve health; for liquid which does not flow stagnates, as do feelings.

The Morgan-Greer Tarot

The Morgan-Greer deck shows the Temperance figure as having a somewhat androgynous appearance, perhaps a symbol of the blend of opposites which this card reflects. As in the Mythic Tarot, one foot is dipped in the pool, the other on dry land, indicating the bridge between mind and body. In the background, behind the angel, a winding road leads into the distance, suggesting that there may be a new route to follow. Meanwhile, the rising sun offers the dawn of new hope in the task of resolving opposites, represented by the twin mountain peaks.

In the Mythic card the irises which grow near the water are a symbol of renewal, and purple is the colour of wisdom.

The triangle positioned on the angel's chest in the Morgan-Greer card (right) is a symbol for the unity of body, mind and spirit.

XIV — TEMPERANCE

The Tarot of the Witches

The star-spangled, blue wings of the Temperance angel in this deck denote the heavens, while her green dress symbolizes the earth on which she stands. She pours a magical rainbow-coloured liquid between two cups, pointing to the constant movement of the past through the present and into the future, the continuity of life and consciousness even over death. It also stands for time as the great equalizer which mixes, in their rightful proportions, the eternal opposites of masculine and feminine, death and life, decay and growth, success and failure.

> STUDENT — *I thought the virtue of Temperance was moderation. How does this fit with this imagery?*

> JULIET — Temperance reflects the need for everything in moderation, because the right mix, symbolized by the carefully blended liquid, is essential for a successful finished product. In partnerships, a balanced input from each partner needs to be combined to produce a healthy relationship as a whole. An unequal contribution from either party does not produce harmony – which is another attribute of the Temperance card.

Le Tarot de Marseilles

This deck shows the familiar image of a winged woman pouring liquid from one jug into another. Temperance in medieval times meant moderation in terms of alcohol consumption, and the mixing of liquid between two jugs may reflect the dilution of wine with water to moderate its effects. The alchemists struggled to discover a way of turning lead into gold or water into wine; and the Christian communion ceremony mixes water and wine to symbolize the water of man and the blood of Christ shed to redeem humanity.

The main two colours of this card are red and blue which again may reflect wine and water, as well as representing unity between other opposites such as masculine and feminine. Temperance represents a constant process of mediation between elements, transforming and blending one into the other as is necessary to achieve a balance. If something is too hot, it must be cooled; if something is too hard, it must be softened; if something is too dry, it must be moistened – so that nothing should exist in an extreme form. Temperance is the card of compromise and moderation which is why it is connected with successful relationships.

The careful pouring of the liquid without spilling any indicates moderation and frugality.

Interpreting TEMPERANCE

Temperance reflects a need for the mixing and blending of opposites. A successful outcome to difficult situations is possible if careful control is used to balance out different elements. This card signifies cooperation and compromise in relationships, with negotiation and sharing of feelings being the key to harmony. In its negative aspect, Temperance can suggest wasting creative energy or repressed stagnant emotions.

The angel in the Marseilles card wears a flower on her forehead with five petals to denote the five senses.

THE DEVIL

Inhibitions, blocks and fears which, once removed, release positive energy

The Devil is traditionally represented as half-man, half-beast, with horns and hooves, seated on a throne with one or two figures chained to him. All the decks discussed here depict him as both bestial and human. The number of this card is fifteen, the components of which, five and one, add up to six, a number which signifies reconciliation of opposites as well as love, which can paradoxically emerge from darkness. The path is sixteen on the Tree of Life, connecting Hod, splendour, and Tifereth, beauty.

THE DEVIL

The Mythic Tarot

The Mythic Tarot shows The Devil as Pan, the Greek goat god. Considered by the Olympian gods to be too ugly and coarse to live in the heavens with them, he ruled as the god of raw nature and sexuality in the hills of Arcadia. According to myth, Pan was not evil, only untamed and natural. He was best known for trying to force his often unwanted sexual attentions upon the Arcadian nymphs. Although the Olympians despised Pan for his gauche ways and crass behaviour, they were not above exploiting him. Apollo the sun god charmed the art of prophecy from him; while Hermes stole his Pan pipe, claimed it as his own and promptly sold it to Apollo. And so it was through deceit and manipulation that the brilliantly accomplished sun god acquired his famed talent in both music and prophecy from the brutish, uncivilized god of nature. The myth illustrates the great potential that resides in the most unusual or unexpected parts of ourselves. We may be so busy looking on the surface of things and being attracted by glittering outward appearances that we do not look deeper at the real gold which may lie within.

| STUDENT | *I have always been rather nervous of drawing The Devil card. Perhaps I need not be afraid of it?* |

The dancing figures in the Mythic card are chained at the neck but their hands are free, symbolizing that bondage to The Devil is a voluntary matter which consciousness can release.

JULIET   Indeed not. Unfortunately, The Devil card has had rather a bad press over the years, mostly because those who are not familiar with the tarot have instantly assumed that he represents evil. In fact, he merely represents the untamed uncivilized aspects of the human psyche which we often tend to fear, feel ashamed of and would prefer not to acknowledge. These include greed, lust, envy, sexual desires, the will to power – in short, those attributes which, in Jungian terminology, comprise the Shadow, our alter ego or darker side. The paradox is that if we deny this darker, less attractive side of ourselves, it causes more problems than if we honestly acknowledge it.

Cary-Yale Visconti Tarocchi

The Visconti deck portrays The Devil as a fierce, forbidding-looking figure with the horns and legs of a goat, bat-like black wings, and talons instead of feet. In his right hand he carries a stick with an open palm on its tip; and his left hand is held up showing the contrast between the true and false hand. Perhaps this represents how deceptive The Devil is, or how difficult it can be to discriminate between what is true and what is false. The symbolism of The Devil connects him with the traditional image of Satan, the great tempter and the embodiment of all that is dark. Yet the other side of Satan was Lucifer, which means the 'bringer of light'. The essence of this card is duality. It is an image of darkness in which light can be found.

The 1JJ Swiss Tarot

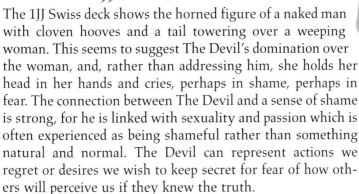

The 1JJ Swiss deck shows the horned figure of a naked man with cloven hooves and a tail towering over a weeping woman. This seems to suggest The Devil's domination over the woman, and, rather than addressing him, she holds her head in her hands and cries, perhaps in shame, perhaps in fear. The connection between The Devil and a sense of shame is strong, for he is linked with sexuality and passion which is often experienced as being shameful rather than something natural and normal. The Devil can represent actions we regret or desires we wish to keep secret for fear of how others will perceive us if they knew the truth.

The Visconti deck's Devil appears to have female breasts which may be an indication of bisexuality.

The Swiss card (above left) portrays a strong naked Devil looking down as if in contempt at the weeping woman.

The Tarot of the Witches

The Witches deck shows a green Devil with one horn of a goat and the other of a ram. His upper body is that of a man but his lower half is of an animal. A few strands of hair which look like snakes protrude from his head. The stone pillar he sits on represents law and order. It seems to be cracking as the flames of hell rise up, perhaps implying that the outer layers of structure and civilization mean nothing to The Devil. The sun and moon appear together in the sky – The Devil seeks mastery over both.

Interpreting THE DEVIL

The Devil represents repressed fears and blocked feelings which, once removed, can release much positive energy. He symbolizes that the time is ripe for a meeting with the darker side of our nature. Although such confrontations may not be very comfortable, they bring great insight and often a release of creative energy once the chains of shame and self-loathing can be broken. The negative interpretation of this card would be repression of the instincts by the intellect, to the seeker's detriment.

In the Witches card The Devil's left foot is hoofed and his right foot clawed, symbolizing his connection with both the animal and the spirit world.

THE TOWER

Rigid or imprisoning structures need to be torn down and replaced with the new

This card traditionally depicts a tower that has been struck by lightning and is in danger of collapse. The decks below show turbulent scenes of human life in danger, with the exception of the Witches deck, in which the landscape is eerily calm. The Tower is number sixteen which breaks down to one and six, which, in turn, add up to seven, the number of positive action. Its path on the Tree of Life is seventeen, linking Netsah, endurance and Hod, splendour.

El Gran Tarot Esoterico

A flaming tower is being attacked on all sides by arrows of white lightning. As lightning strikes the heart of the tower, people are flung from the upper parts of the building. It is clear from the imagery of this card that something is being destroyed, but exactly what that might be is a subject for interpretation. The Tower is the only man-made symbol in the tarot; all the other images are human or planetary. This may suggest that what needs to be challenged may be man-made too. Some writers have related this card to The Tower of Babel built by Noah's descendants, angry with God for having destroyed their ancestors in the Great Flood. In their arrogance, they decided to construct a tower tall enough to reach heaven, so they might invade and take their revenge on God. Naturally their inflated plot failed and God punished those involved by making each of them speak a different language, causing chaos and confusion. Ever since then verbal communication among men has been complicated. The Tower is often seen as reflecting false pride or boastful ideas which need to be corrected.

The Grand Esoteric card signals freedom from limitation as the tall, narrow and imprisoning tower is shattered.

STUDENT — *This looks a very uncomfortable card. Is it a 'bad' one?*

JULIET — I don't like the idea of any tarot card being looked upon as 'bad'. Their energy is neutral; it is what one does with that energy which makes it 'bad' or 'good'. In fact, my way of interpreting The Tower is as a cleansing, cathartic experience, because it provides an opportunity for clearing out the old. Anything that has outlived its usefulness can be dispensed with under the influences of The Tower. It is the right time for tearing down false beliefs, for this card indicates an appropriate moment for new, healthy structures to be built. It can also represent the separation process which occurs in adolescence when parental values are examined and often rejected in favour of new ideas. This can sometimes bring great disruption in its wake, but is usually in response to too much rigidity.

The Morgan-Greer Tarot

A fierce storm is raging and the tower is struck by lightning. A man and woman are falling from the battlements, which suggests that neither sex is exempt from the changes this card represents. Waves lick at the tower's base, flames pour from the roof and windows, and dark storm clouds gather in the sky – the natural elements of water, fire and air are represented – the fourth element, earth, is symbolized by the structure of the tower itself. There is a reminder that no matter how wonderful and ingenious man's creations may be, the forces of nature are always more powerful. The lightning flash has long been thought of as a symbol of enlightenment – the bolt from Zeus, and the overpowering light of truth which is prominent in Tantric Buddhism – the flash of enlightenment which changes everything.

The Tarot of the Witches

The scene depicted in the Witches deck is eerily calm compared to the mayhem in the other Tower cards shown here. No figures appear, and only the top of the stone tower is lifted by a single fork of white lightning. The colour white suggests that enlightenment and insight may triumph over ignorance and darkness. The dark clouds are clearing and the new moon appears, indicating the beginning of a new phase.

The barren trees at the foot of The Tower in the Witches card (left) stand in a carefully tended field which symbolizes that the difficulties of the past may be overcome by better prospects for the future.

The elements tear at man's creation, demonstrating nature's triumph over mankind's arrogance.

Cary-Yale Visconti Tarocchi

In the Visconti deck, the top of the tower is knocked off under the blast of fire from the heavens. The crown of the building symbolizes the higher consciousness; thus the flash of light slices through the structures of the ego. The heavenly lightning is seen as divine inspiration and understanding. The overall picture reveals that human existence is a constant state of change and upheaval and that no human construction can survive if it cannot adapt to prevailing circumstances.

Interpreting THE TOWER

In a reading, The Tower indicates a time of abrupt changes. Old ideas suddenly seem outdated and inappropriate. Existing forms need to be broken down in order to make way for new ones. The seeker is often required to examine his or her beliefs and ideologies and must be prepared to strip away anything which is no longer relevant. Positively, this is a time which can be very liberating; yet on the negative side, the clearing away of old habits and structures could be rather alarming for the seeker, leaving him or her feeling vulnerable.

The Visconti card shows a crowned man at the foot of the image indicating that no one, whether king or pauper, can escape change.

THE STAR

Hope, promise, renewal, and light after darkness

The most common depiction of The Star is a maiden pouring water from two jugs freely into a pool, with a star overhead. The Rider-Waite and Ukiyoe decks follow this imagery while the Mythic Tarot shows the Star of Hope. The Haindl deck also departs from traditional images by depicting a woman washing her hair. The card's number is seventeen: the figures one and seven combining to make eight, which stands for rebirth, renewal and baptism. The Star is also connected with the seven days of creation and the eighth day of regeneration. On the Tree of Life its path is eighteen, linking Netsah, endurance and Yesod, foundation.

The Haindl Tarot

The Haindl deck portrays The Star as a cloaked woman bending over a stony waterfall washing her hair, a symbol of her unity with the earth, suggesting that earth will cleanse herself of injustice and hatred. She is Gaia, the ancient goddess of the earth, the Mother of Life. There is no vegetation around her, only rock and water which were earth's original substances.

The Star is an image of renewal and hope, so the message offered by the Haindl deck is that, as earth's children are faced with the decision between destruction and a respect for existence, they will ultimately, somehow, choose life. In the grey sky above, seven small stars gleam softly, seven being the number of progress; while a double star shines out in the centre, making up eight, the number for woman and new life.

The Star

The Ukiyoe Tarot

The Ukiyoe deck shows a woman in an everyday kimono wearing a red sash to indicate creativity, while the willow trees in the distance denote patience and perseverance, virtues which are essential when producing anything that is worthwhile. The liquid she pours freely into the river may be sake, returning a distillation of rice back to the river so that it may, in turn, flow on to nurture and feed the next crop. Eight stars of inspiration encircle her head, symbolizing divine guidance, hope and promise – a light to steer by in the dark of night.

Gaia's hair blends into the water, and her grey dress melts into the rock, showing her to be as old as time.

The high mountain peaks in the background in the Ukiyoe card (right) indicate inspiration and desire for achievement.

THE STAR

The Mythic Tarot

The Mythic Tarot uses the Greek myth of Pandora to illustrate the message of The Star. After Prometheus had stolen divine fire from the gods, Zeus decided to torment humankind as a punishment for having accepted the stolen gift. Together, the Olympian gods produced the first woman, Pandora, making her beautiful, wise and fruitful. They offered her as bride to Prometheus' brother, giving her a chest which they warned her not to open. However, Pandora, being as curious as she was beautiful, opened the box. No sooner had she done so than all the spites and ills, such as madness, pain, vice and old age, flew out in the form of insects, covering the earth and bringing terrible afflictions to humankind. Only Hope remained, which Prometheus had slipped into the box before his torture. He was afraid that, without him to protect them, humankind would never survive the torments of the gods.

The chest from Zeus is similar to the apple in the Garden of Eden. It is both irresistible and forbidden; it contains both knowledge of the reality of human existence, and one of the most precious and resilient qualities of the human spirit – hope.

THE STAR

Although the air is thick with the ugly spites, Pandora keeps her eyes raised to the Star of Hope.

The Rider-Waite Tarot

The Rider-Waite deck depicts The Star as a maiden; her nakedness symbolizes truth, while her youth suggests renewal. She pours the Water of Life freely from two pitchers: from one it splashes into a pool, while from the other it flows onto the land in five streams, representing the five senses. The figure may represent Ganymede, the Greek cupbearer whose constellation is the astrological sign of Aquarius the Water-carrier, while the bird perched on the distant tree is a symbol of air, the element of Aquarius.

The seven small stars might be the seven planets of the ancient world; or possibly stand for the Pleiades, the seven mythical sisters who were turned into stars and therefore symbolize immortality; and they have also been connected to the seven ages of man. The central, eighth star reflects the potential for transcending normal earthly limitations. While the more common five-pointed star is a symbol of rebirth, protection and salvation, this star is connected with Venus, the morning star, which brings with it the promise of a new day, just as the biblical Star of Bethlehem signaled the birth of Jesus, carrying the message, 'the Way, the Truth and the Light'. The birth, death and resurrection of Christ brought new trust and confidence in the potential for divine forgiveness and immortality and so, in turn, it brought hope.

XVII

THE STAR.

The bird in the background of the Rider-Waite card is a symbol of the spirit's ability to rise to higher levels of consciousness.

Interpreting THE STAR

The Star in a layout represents a positive outlook and a source of optimism and expectation. It indicates a sense of purpose and a trust in the ultimate goodness in life. Stars in the heavens have always been associated with hope and wonder; and in the tarot The Star provides that magic and belief which can keep us going, even when things are difficult. Its negative interpretation would be self-doubt, and a lack of faith and trust.

THE MOON

A period of illusion, uncertainty and fluctuation

For The Moon card, many decks show a full moon with the hounds of the underworld baying beneath, while others show lovers pledging their mutual affection under its pale light. The Ukiyoe and the Rider-Waite decks use a similar theme of two dogs, pillars and mountain peaks, while the 1JJ Swiss Tarot depicts lovers in the moonlight. The Mythic Tarot departs from traditional imagery to show the three faces and phases of the moon. The number of this card is eighteen, and one and eight combine to give nine, the number of solitude and vulnerability. Its path on the Tree of Life is nineteen, linking Malkuth, kingdom, with Netsah, endurance.

In the Rider-Waite card a narrow road winds between the two sinister looking towers indicating that the path to understanding is neither clear nor easy.

The Rider-Waite Tarot

A dog and a wolf bark at the moon while a crayfish struggles to reach dry land from the depths of the pool. The crayfish may originally have been a crab, the astrological sign of Cancer, which is ruled by the moon. The crab is a creature which belongs equally to the land and the sea, and constantly moves between those mediums. This perpetual shifting of the crab is like the movement between the conscious and unconscious mind, thought and feeling.

The moon shines down revealing her three faces, new, full and old. It was once believed that the moon was the womb from which all life sprang, but equally she was the tomb to which all life eventually returned; hence her dual nature as both giver and taker of all existence. The Moon is connected with the feminine cycle, the tides and the natural waxing and waning rhythms of life.

STUDENT | *I have heard The Moon is not a very pleasant card to turn up in a reading. Is that true?*

JULIET | The older traditional interpretations tend to concentrate on only one aspect of The Moon, that is the dark side. However, The Moon does have three phases and three faces. The waning moon represents those older, traditional ways of interpreting the card, which include deceit, disillusion and loss of direction. But there are other faces to choose from, namely: the new moon, which, like The Star, represents promise; and the full moon, which stands for fertility and fulfilment. The Moon is a symbol of something which is ever changing yet its cycle is constant and steady – even as it changes, so it stays the same. The overall meaning of this card is that there is likely to be a period of flux and change in the seeker's life and that nothing is straightforward or clear. This is neither good nor bad, but can be confusing for the seeker.

The Ukiyoe Tarot

The Moon rules the night, the time of darkness, sleep and dreams. A brilliant full moon shines over twin pagodas, one black, one white. The theme of pairs recurs: two pagodas, two dogs, two banks, two trees; reflecting the constant tension between the opposites in life: day and night, light and dark, strength and weakness, masculine and feminine, conscious and unconscious. The crab is swimming upstream towards a lake, which is not its natural habitat. This may symbolize the notion that to achieve consciousness is a struggle and that there is a continual conflict between conscious and unconscious desires.

The 1JJ Swiss Tarot

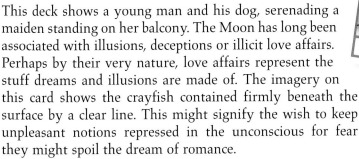

This deck shows a young man and his dog, serenading a maiden standing on her balcony. The Moon has long been associated with illusions, deceptions or illicit love affairs. Perhaps by their very nature, love affairs represent the stuff dreams and illusions are made of. The imagery on this card shows the crayfish contained firmly beneath the surface by a clear line. This might signify the wish to keep unpleasant notions repressed in the unconscious for fear they might spoil the dream of romance.

Divided in two, the Swiss card (left) makes a clear distinction between the conscious and the unconscious realms of existence.

The Ukiyoe card shows a bright red crab, the colour of conscious desire.

The Mythic Tarot

This card shows a three-headed woman crowned with the moon in its three phases representing the three phases of womanhood: virgin, mother and elder. The new moon is often associated with Persephone, the virgin, full of possibility and potential; the full moon with her mother, Demeter, the woman fulfilled; finally, the dark moon is connected with Hecate, daughter of Hera, who infuriated her mother by stealing her rouge. Hecate fled to earth taking refuge in the home of a woman who had just had a baby. Soiled with the blood of childbirth, she was sent to the underworld to wash away her stain in the river Styx. However, she liked the underworld so much she stayed there and became one of its rulers. Her dog, the three-headed hound of hell and guardian of the underworld, stands for past, present and future.

THE MOON

Interpreting THE MOON

In a reading, The Moon suggests that a time of uncertainty and confusion is likely. There is fluctuation and change; yet it does not have to be negative. A sense of gestation is present, something is growing silently and secretly and when the time is ripe it will be revealed. The inner confusion should be allowed rather than 'solved' – confusion can be creative and The Moon points to a potential for creativity. Solutions to problems are more likely to be found through dreams and feelings than in logic and reason.

The Mythic goddess stands in the Pool of Forgetfulness in the underworld, indicating that the wealth contained in dreams is easily forgotten.

THE SUN

Cheerfulness, prosperity, energy and optimism

The Sun is traditionally portrayed in the tarot as a child or children in a flower garden. The Visconti and Rider-Waite decks both depict a child riding a white horse, while the Morgan-Greer Tarot shows a boy and girl facing each other in a walled garden, similar to that in the Rider-Waite deck. The Haindl deck breaks with tradition by portraying a blazing sun above a surreal landscape. The Sun's number is nineteen which breaks down to one and nine, the total of which is ten, the number of attainment and completion; this breaks down further to one plus nought, making one, the number of will and self-assertion. Its path on the Tree of Life is twenty, linking Yesod, foundation, and Hod, splendour.

The Cary-Yale Visconti Tarocchi

A naked youth rides a white horse through the sky carrying a disembodied golden head crowned with sunrays. In early Greek mythology, the sun god Helios would drive a horse-drawn sun chariot across the skies. In this way, Helios provided the warmth and light needed by those who lived on earth – symbolized by the cities, fields and seas below the horse. Later, Apollo, the dazzling god of music, art and civilization, was worshipped as the sun god. He was also a healer whose gold-tipped arrows could drive away pain and sickness – but his arrows could kill as well as cure if Apollo was vexed.

The Haindl Tarot

The Sun card in the Haindl deck shows a scene which looks like a fantasy world, certainly like nothing we are familiar with in nature. A red rose is on the point of unfolding its petals, revealing it to be at the height of its beauty. The sun, made up of a tight coil of spirals, shines brightly in a darkened sky. The image seems to reflect a vision of nature rather than trying to represent nature itself.

The Sun

The Haindl card figures a circle with a dot in its centre, the astrological glyph for the sun which represents the heart of the psyche.

The golden head in the Visconti card resembles the sun god Apollo.

STUDENT	*The Sun card always looks so cheerful. Would you say this was one of the best cards in the deck?*
JULIET	I don't like to think of any card as better or worse than any other and each card has its own unique and absolutely necessary place in

the deck. Having said that, however, there is no doubt that The Sun is usually very welcome in a spread as it radiates optimism and positive energy. Its great feature is that of clarity and vision, and the light it can shed on darkness or uncertainty. The Moon feels confusing and unpredictable while with The Sun you really feel you know where you are.

The Rider-Waite Tarot

The Rider-Waite Tarot shows a beaming naked child riding on the same white horse that previously carried Death in this deck. The Sun is an image of rebirth: after setting each dusk, it rises again every morning and lives to mark another day. At the midsummer solstice the sun shines out triumphantly and symbolizes a strong, mighty god; but in the depths of winter he is the weak, dying god, who will be reborn as a little child at the winter solstice. A sense of sheer joy and celebration is evident in this image which seems to radiate enthusiasm and pleasure. The Rider-Waite card portrays the sun with straight and wavy lines shining from it, representing both the positive and negative aspects of his rays. In cooler climates the sun was worshipped as a source of light and life and was welcomed as beneficent. In hotter climes, however, he brought heat and drought and was feared as the deity who could parch and destroy crops. The tarot constantly reminds us of the need for balance and that too much emphasis on any one thing is not desirable.

The Morgan-Greer Tarot

Two children face each other with a huge orange sun behind them. They represent the two sides of the psyche, ready to become whole and integrated. There is a boy, who stands for thought, action and the masculine, and a girl who represents feeling, intuition and the feminine. Apollo the sun god is connected with the arts, civilization and the intellect; his sister Artemis is associated with the feminine intuition of the moon. These twin deities of the sun and moon are inextricably linked, one rules by day, the other by night. Their masculine and feminine qualities are not found in men or women exclusively, rather they are both found in both sexes – as the mixing and merging of the opposites produce a whole. The wall can be seen as a symbol of containment – as the circle of the zodiac around which the sun makes its yearly journey, or as the physical body which contains the spirit of each human being.

The red banner in the Rider-Waite card symbolizes liberation from darkness, just as the sun frees the world from night each morning.

The beautiful sunflowers which grow around the children signify the sun's life-giving generosity.

Interpreting THE SUN

The Sun card indicates a good time for action and confident planning for the future, as things can be seen clearly and ideas formed consciously. It suggests energy, strength, good health and a positive attitude. It gives cheer to the surrounding cards in a reading, radiating joy, optimism and strong friendships, and augurs well for love and peace of mind. The negative slant to this card might be a lack of sensitivity, a tendency to be over-confident or arrogant, and a lack of awareness of limitations.

JUDGEMENT

Completion of the karmic cycle; reaping rewards, or otherwise, for past actions

The imagery of the Judgement card varies comparatively little across the different decks. Traditionally the picture reveals an angel or heavenly figure blowing a trumpet, calling the dead to rise. The Russian, Ukiyoe and Rider-Waite decks follow this imagery with the dead rising out of their graves; and the Mythic Tarot depicts Hermes in the underworld inviting the dead to shake off their burial shrouds. The card's number is twenty and its figures, two and nought, add up to two, a number which represents opposites, in this case of life and death. Its path on the Tree of Life is twenty-one, linking Hod, splendour, and Malkuth, kingdom.

The Ukiyoe Tarot

The image on this deck is of three souls rising from a traditional Japanese stone graveyard, while Kwannon, the goddess of mercy, floats on a cloud overhead. In Buddhist teaching, Kwannon is the deity who guides souls to Utopia, and her grace is prayed for. Buddhist doctrine teaches that she (who started out as a male deity but was later thought of as female) was the Buddha's spiritual son, born from a tear that Buddha wept when he saw the suffering of the world. The three souls in this image are moving towards their next incarnation, praying that their rebirth will be in the Pure Land, free from human suffering and the torment of earthly life. Before each soul's fate can be decided, each must first be judged and assessed in the light of his life. All actions, whatever they may be, have a price, and Judgement symbolizes the Day of Reckoning.

The Russian Tarot of St Petersburg

A trumpet blast awakens the dead, the heavenly sound inspiring the man, woman and child to rise from their graves, yearning for higher things. The cross on the flag symbolizes the joining together of what were previously separate. This card has been linked with karmic law: each man's life and actions on earth are judged after death and, depending on those actions, he is either rewarded by passing through to nirvana or punished by being thrust back on the wheel of life. The Catholic Church suggests that souls not yet fit for heaven but not deserving hell must suffer in purgatory until such time as the soul is ready for paradise.

The goddess in the Ukiyoe card is holding prayer beads in one hand and a wish-fulfilling gem in the other.

The angel in the Russian card (right) stands on a crescent moon, symbolizing a new phase or beginning.

The Mythic Tarot

The Mythic Tarot uses Hermes in his role as psychopomp (meaning 'guide of souls') and as the messenger heralding rebirth. According to Greek mythology, the messenger-god Hermes had an additional role as a deity of the underworld, leading the dying to Hades. Three stern judges, Minos, Rhadamanthus and Aeacus, who were distinguished for their justice on earth, judged the souls Hermes brought before them. Hades itself had a dark and a light side: while the wicked were severely punished by the Furies, those who had lived virtuous lives passed into the blissful Elysian fields where they lived the joys of life once again.

STUDENT *Is The Magician linked with the Judgement card as they are both connected with the Greek god Hermes?*

JULIET Well it is certainly interesting that The Magician starts the trump cards (The Fool, of course, is unnumbered and is able to fit in anywhere) while Judgement is the penultimate card, the one which leads on to completion in The World. I like to think of Hermes as being the guide who leads men through their lives, as symbolized in the procession of trumps. All aspects of life are covered: parents, love, war, moral lessons, disappointment, change, death, enlightenment and, ultimately, Hermes leads them out of the underworld to a new stage of life.

Hermes' golden caduceus, entwined with the twin snakes of opposites, would touch the eyes of the dying to bring blessed sleep before ushering them into Hades.

The Rider-Waite Tarot

A golden-haired angel appears from the clouds sounding his mighty trumpet. From the trumpet hangs a white flag with a red cross: the central point at which the lines cross tells that the way towards knowledge and spiritual growth is through the joining of opposing forces to form a third, higher entity. Naked figures rise up from their open coffins, their arms raised in a gesture of joyful liberation. The figures are naked because their worldly attire is no longer necessary; they have undergone their spiritual rebirth and are now ready and open for new life. The angel is often identified with the Archangel Michael who led the forces of light against the darkness in the war of heaven. With a similar role to Hermes the psychopomp, Michael is a guide of Christian souls and will be the Awakener on the Final Day of Judgement when all men and women will be examined and their lives evaluated.

Interpreting JUDGEMENT

When the Judgement card turns up in a reading, it suggests that the time is ripe for an evaluation of past events. It is a time of consolidation, of summing up, and of forming conclusions, a time to reap the rewards or pay the penalty for past actions. Judgement indicates the end of a chapter, and therefore marks a new beginning; but in-between lies a confrontation with the consequences of past choices and actions. Positively, it suggests joy in achievement, and negatively, reflects regret over wasted opportunities or ill-advised actions.

The dark tombs in the Rider-Waite card suggest life without meaning or understanding.

THE WORLD

The realization of a prize or goal; success, triumph, achievement

One of the most traditional images of this card is of an oval wreath inside which a figure dances. Often four heads occupy the corners. The Grand Esoteric and the Ukiyoe decks follow this traditional imagery, while the Visconti deck depicts a crown, and the Witches' deck uses a vision of planet earth. The number of the card is twenty-one, two and one combining to make three, the number of creation and integration. Its path on the Tree of Life is twenty-two, linking Malkuth, kingdom, and Yesod, foundation.

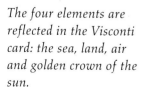

Cary-Yale Visconti Tarocchi

A richly attired woman emerges from a golden crown, unfolding into blue-ribboned clouds, which in Renaissance art represented the vehicles of divine personages. She may stand for Fame, holding a trumpet in one hand and a crown in the other. The traditional interpretation of this card is a prize or reward, and it appears in this image that the crown is being offered as the longed-for goal. The journey is at an end; The Fool has become the master. Beneath the crown lies a perfect world of castles, fields and ships, which has an almost fairy-tale quality. The city may represent one of the ideal cities where perfection and wholeness were thought to reign eternally, such as the holy city of Jerusalem, the Celtic Avalon, or the classical garden of the Hesperides.

STUDENT	*This is the best card in the tarot isn't it?*

| JULIET | Supposedly so, although, as I have said, I do not consider any one of the cards to be 'better' than |

another. Nevertheless, The World does signify a time of fruition which is always satisfying. However, remember that over the brow of the hill lies another journey. No sooner have you finished one project than you must start thinking about the next!

The Tarot of the Witches

This surreal image portrays the planet earth, as viewed from space. A large tear of sorrow falls from her eye, yet there is the hint of a faint smile on her lips. She weeps for the destruction of life through violence, hate and greed; yet there is still hope for salvation. Seven stars, which may represent the seven ancient planets, and a

The four elements are reflected in the Visconti card: the sea, land, air and golden crown of the sun.

The Witches card (right) shows the earth hanging over the desolate landscape of another planet. Perhaps this is a warning as to the possible fate of our world.

XXI

THE WORLD

sun encircle the world. A small tree grows from one continent. This is the Tree of Knowledge which represents the joys and achievement still possible for humankind. A smouldering volcano suggests the sadness that is so often part of human experience. At the top and bottom of the earth are ice caps, reminding us of the coldness and isolation of a world without compassion.

El Gran Tarot Esoterico

A curious figure stands in a gold circle of flowers symbolizing success and completion. It appears to have female breasts, but also has male genitals, indicating that the figure may be a hermaphrodite – a symbol of unity between the opposites. The sun and moon both appear as images of male and female with the central figure indicating the result of their union. Appearing in each corner are the heads of the four creatures which appeared in the Old-Testament prophet Ezekiel's vision of God – the bull, the lion, the eagle and the man. These four were also known as the 'guardians of heaven' and represent the four fixed zodiacal signs, the four elements and the four seasons, as follows: the bull, Taurus, earth, spring; the lion, Leo, fire, summer; the eagle, Scorpio, water, autumn; the man, Aquarius, air, winter.

The central figure may represent the quintessence of the alchemists – the four elements blended together to form a perfect fifth. However, the sense of completion and perfection that this card shows cannot last indefinitely, so the central figure becomes the foetus in the womb, waiting to be reborn again as The Fool. The wheel turns, and the journey starts again.

The Ukiyoe Tarot

A woman draped in a scarf stands in a wreath made up of morning glories, the Japanese flower of mortality. A white and red butterfly hovers over the flowers. In Japanese legend, the human soul will take the form of a butterfly and return to earth to enjoy the pleasures of nectar and sunshine. As in the Grand Esoteric deck, each corner of the card carries a creature: the ox, symbol of earth, a strong, hardworking beast; the lion, a fire creature who guards the sacred shrines; the eagle, reflecting the air and spiritual aspiration; while Kwannon, the goddess of mercy, reflects the element of water. These are slightly different to the more traditional correspondences used in the Grand Esoteric deck.

The white stole, a symbol of purity, hangs round the Grand-Esoteric figure's neck in equal lengths, with the same star on each side suggesting equality and perfect harmony.

Interpreting THE WORLD

The World is a card of success, achievement and fulfilment, and is therefore to be welcomed in a reading. It suggests the completion of a stage or phase in life, and – on a cosmic level – carries the suggestion of self-integration and harmony with nature and the universe. In Jungian language, this is the realization of the Self. On a more mundane level, however, it is connected with the moment of attainment and the attendant sense of satisfaction.

The beautiful landscape in the Ukiyoe card represents the Pure Land, the goal at the end of many incarnations.

CHAPTER THREE
THE MINOR ARCANA

The fifty-six cards of the Minor Arcana are made up of four suits, each including the cards Ace to Ten and four court cards: Page, Knight, Queen and King. These form the prototype for our modern-day playing cards – Cups, Wands, Swords and Pentacles each became Hearts, Clubs, Spades and Diamonds respectively. Modern decks have also dropped the Page completely, and Jack is now equivalent to the Knight. Some tarot decks, however, use Prince and Princess cards as the Page and Knight. Older tarot decks had no pictures on the Minor Arcana pip cards so, when the Rider-Waite deck was created in 1910 with pictorial pip cards, it started a new trend. It is obviously easier to associate and remember the divinatory meanings when there is a picture to use as a memory aid.

Each suit of the Minor Arcana can be connected with a number of associations. Primarily, the Cups are connected with feelings and love; the Wands with intuition and creative energy; the Swords are linked to the intellect; and the Pentacles to the material world. The suits also have associations with the divisions of medieval society; the four sacred objects found in the Grail castle of Arthurian legend; and the magic emblems of Celtic myth. Indeed, the four suits could also illustrate the four elements – water, fire, air and earth – and the four compass points – north, east, south and west. There is no definitive answer as to which interpretation is the 'right' one, and it is part of the tarot's magical, elusive fascination that we cannot absolutely track it down and categorize it. Yet, interestingly enough, although the designs of the images have altered over the years to reflect the styles of their time, the tarot deck as a whole has remained more or less intact since the earliest decks.

THE SUIT OF
～ CUPS ～

The suit of Cups is connected primarily with feelings, emotions and love. One of its many other associations is with the church or clergy, as a division of medieval society. Another is as one of the Grail Hallows, the Cup being a symbol of the Grail itself, the chalice used by Christ at the Last Supper. The Cups have also been connected with the cauldron of the Dagda, the Celtic father god. This magic cauldron was always full and, no matter how many ate or drank from it, its supply was never exhausted; it could even bring the dead back to life. In addition, this suit is linked with the element of water, from which all life was thought to have sprung. In turn, the water signs in astrology can be connected, in Jungian psychology, with the feeling function, reflecting the emotional tone Cups bring to a reading.

Non-pictorial cards from the suit of Cups are shown above, belonging to the Marseilles, Swiss, Visconti, Witches, Esoteric and Ukiyoe decks (left to right).

∼ ACE OF CUPS ∼

The beginning of a relationship, a surge of emotion, joy

The dove of peace fluttering behind the cup represents feelings and spiritual values, and the water lily below is a sign of emotional development.

The Morgan-Greer Tarot

The Ace is the number of pure energy, undiluted and vital; thus the Ace of Cups indicates a powerful source of emotional energy and a time for new beginnings in the realm of feelings and relationships. A hand reaches out from the clouds to offer the golden cup filled with promise and hope. Five streams of liquid overflow from the chalice symbolizing the five senses as well as the abundance this card represents.

Interpreting the ACE OF CUPS

The Ace of Cups suggests a time of emotional and spiritual nourishment. Traditionally it is associated with love, marriage and motherhood, yet it also signifies a fruitful, creative period full of potential and possibilities for personal projects to be conceived. The passion of the Ace contains a potent energy which can result in new relationships or love affairs.

∼ TWO OF CUPS ∼

Friendship, partnership, reconciliation of opposites

The Haindl Tarot

The Haindl deck has assigned this card the first hexagram of the I Ching (in the bottom left-hand corner) which means 'The Creative'. The Two of Cups is traditionally associated with forming or committing to a partnership or relationship. This is subtly different to the previous card – the Ace of Cups suggests the potential for relationship, while the Two indicates the existence of a partnership into which time and energy need to be poured.

Behind the two golden cups with stars sparkling above them stands a beautiful peacock as a symbol of rebirth, balance and the fantasy needed in love and relationships.

Love
Two of Cups

Interpreting the TWO OF CUPS

The Two of Cups signals a time for cooperation and compromise within a partnership, whether a love affair or a platonic relationship. It can indicate the end of rivalry, bringing a period of reconciliation and a platform from which to work. Ideas can be exchanged and common goals worked out. This card can suggest a happy balance between spiritual and physical love.

~ THREE OF CUPS ~
A time for rejoicing and celebration

Here the marriage of Eros and Psyche describes the moment of joy and sense of achievement the Three of Cups suggests.

The Mythic Tarot

Three is the number of initial completion, suggesting that the ground laid out in the Ace and the Two comes to fruition in the Three. In these terms, the image of a wedding used here is apt, for the ceremony itself is the culmination of the betrothal, the first phase of the relationship. However, it is only the starting point for the marriage; the wedding is a chapter of celebration and rejoicing, but is only a small part of the whole story.

Interpreting the THREE OF CUPS

The Three of Cups signifies a happy event of any nature. It may literally represent a wedding or the birth of a child, or may signify a time of festivity and joy which punctuates life from time to time. There is a sense of achievement and reward, which can also indicate the healing of wounds, emotional or spiritual, and a return to health.

~ FOUR OF CUPS ~
Boredom, discontent, dissatisfaction

The Norse Tarot

This card is sometimes known as the card of 'divine discontent'. It appears that the seeker has a lot to be pleased about but is focusing only on the things that are wrong. There is a sense of apathy and depression which can lead to becoming stuck in a negative pattern of thinking. A useful, albeit somewhat clichéd, question illustrated in this deck might be, 'Do you think of the cup as half-empty or half-full?'

The woman is young and beautiful with three full cups before her. Yet she only concentrates on the empty cup in her hand.

Interpreting the FOUR OF CUPS

The Four of Cups indicates a time of boredom and frustration. It suggests an inability to make use of the possibilities available and a tendency to focus heavily on difficulties and obstacles. It does not mean that life is any more difficult or trying than usual, it is just that the seeker feels that it is. This card warns against pessimistic attitudes.

~ FIVE OF CUPS ~

Regret over past actions, sorrow, melancholy

A sombre figure in a black cloak of mourning weeps over three spilled cups. Behind him stand two upright cups which suggest that all is not lost.

The Rider-Waite Tarot

The Five, in the tarot, is a number of uncertainty and change. The Five of Cups suggests a change in relationships: perhaps the overturned goblets symbolize a loss or disappointment which is hard to bear. However, the two cups still standing upright and full represent the positive side to the situation which can be built on. The river in the distance reminds us that feelings must continue to flow, for stagnation leads to despair.

Interpreting the FIVE OF CUPS

Something is lost – there is a period of change which may cause sadness and regret. However, as well as mourning the loss, something salvageable in the situation needs to be addressed. Change is rarely easy but often necessary, and may only be understood with hindsight. While this card might indicate a difficult time, it also offers hope for the future.

DILLONS THE BOOKSTORE
22 Sidney Street
CAMBRIDGE
CB2 3HG
Tel: 01223 351 688
VAT No. 710 6311 84

151 CASH-1   2440 0075 004
RSTANDING THE   QTY 1   10.99
          TOTAL   10.99

ASH   11.00
     CHANGE   .01
ANK YOU FOR SHOPPING AT DILLONS

          19.01.99 18:23

~ SIX OF CUPS ~

Past efforts bring rewards in the present

of St Petersburg

rmony and balance; the e equal blend of mascu- x of Cups suggests that happy fruition. Each step holds one or two cups olize creative and loving leading to rewards both in the present and for the future. This card links past with present and brings hope for good times ahead.

A young couple arrange flowers together in a jewelled goblet. Five other goblets, containing bouquets of brightly coloured blooms, sit on the steps leading up to them.

Six of Cups

Interpreting the SIX OF CUPS

This is the card of memory and nostalgia. It suggests a tendency to idealize or 'live' in the past, which might indicate a lack of energy invested in present and future projects. Alternatively, it can suggest that a long-held dream or ambition can be achieved. It might mean a chance reunion with a childhood friend or old sweetheart.

~ SEVEN OF CUPS ~

Creativity and talent in abundance, confusion of choices

Seven cups rise from the clouds to reveal strange and wonderful visions. They are dreams – 'castles in the air' – which must be made actual in the real world.

The Morgan-Greer Tarot

The Seven of Cups is a card of choices and the difficulties which inevitably arise when making decisions. So many wonderful opportunities rise out of the cups depicted here – the wreath representing success, the jewels symbolizing wealth, the castle indicating power, the dragon of adventure, and the snake of knowledge. In addition, a face and a mask also appear, suggesting the opportunity to connect the inner self with the outer persona.

Interpreting the SEVEN OF CUPS

This card represents great mental and imaginative activity. Choices and decisions need to be made but, with so much to choose from, great care and consideration is needed. There is a danger that the desires will remain dreams and fantasies rather than being made real – this abundance of creative and artistic talent should not be wasted.

~ EIGHT OF CUPS ~

Time to let go of the past

The Rider-Waite Tarot

The Eight is the number of death and rebirth. This card symbolizes the need to abandon old ways, and to face fears of encountering the unknown. The precision of the stacked cups indicates that much effort and interest has gone into their placement, and yet it seems not enough. Perhaps the traveller has left them behind out of disappointment, perhaps they did not fulfil his hopes and expectations. The death of the old brings new life.

A cloaked man heads towards the barren mountains, turning his back on eight cups. The Moon, shown in its full and waning quarters, signifies something coming to an end.

Interpreting the EIGHT OF CUPS

The Eight of Cups suggests that the time is ripe to abandon the past; old ways of doing things are no longer working. This card indicates that despite the effort and attention that has been invested in past ventures, whether relationships or creative endeavours, they are no longer working. The cups are full and upright but the seeker has outgrown them.

~ NINE OF CUPS ~
Satisfaction, emotional fulfilment, sensuality

NINE OF CUPS

Eros and Psyche are reunited in love. They raise their cups of love and make their promise to one another, this time with the blessing of Aphrodite.

The Mythic Tarot

The Nine of Cups indicates indulgence and gratification on all sensual levels. The image on this card is of Eros and Psyche meeting again after a period of deep unhappiness and loss. They remake their wedding vows, but this time with a difference – they face one another truthfully knowing their virtues and their vices. The image is one of emotional satisfaction. Their former enemy, Aphrodite, is now their benefactor.

Interpreting the NINE OF CUPS

The Nine of Cups has been thought of traditionally as the 'wish card'. It suggests that a desire or wish of paramount importance to the seeker can be actualized. It is not a card of deep spiritual advancement but rather indicates a time for sensual enjoyment and pleasure – for deep satisfaction, emotionally, physically and materially.

~ TEN OF CUPS ~
Contentment, peace and harmony in relationships

The Rider-Waite Tarot

The Ten of Cups is an image of ongoing contentment. The Nine reveals a sense of ecstasy which cannot endure, while the Ten shows hope for lasting joy. The image is of the family in harmony: the man and woman, boy and girl, symbolizing equality. The dancing children communicate hope for future generations, and their entwined arms stand for cooperation. The house in the distance represents the security they have worked for together.

A happy family scene with an embracing couple stretching their arms out in joy at the sight of the rainbow, a symbol of promise and hope.

Interpreting the TEN OF CUPS

The Ten of Cups suggests happiness and contentment in a relationship. It is a card which indicates good fortune as a result of striving and struggling rather than through sheer luck or opportunity. This hard work, both past and present, will require constant endeavour if the successful partnership is to continue – its rewards are worth the effort.

~ PAGE OF CUPS ~

New beginnings, the birth of a child or budding relationship

The Page of Cups is shown as a Valet carrying a cup and an arrow. He represents potential in the world of dreams, fantasies and creativity.

VALET OF CUPS

The Tarot of the Witches

Across the suits, the Pages act as messengers: they bring ideas or news. In many decks they are symbolized by young people or children, like the solemn young man shown here, for they represent potential and possibilities. The Page of Cups brings possibilities in the realm of feelings and the arrow he carries symbolizes the shaft of love. He represents the innocence, sensitivity and promise of a child whose potential needs careful nurturing.

Interpreting the PAGE OF CUPS

The most traditional meaning of this card is news of a birth. This may be literally the birth of a child, but it can also indicate the birth of creative ideas or new feelings. In this respect it could suggest a relationship in its earliest stages, which requires the most tender care as does anything young and delicate in order to bring out its best.

~ KNIGHT OF CUPS ~

Love, dreams, art

The Swiss 1JJ Tarot

The Knight of Cups is associated with love. He was traditionally said to bring a proposition of some kind, such as a proposal of marriage. All the Knights travel on horseback as they all signify a transition period. The Knight of Cups therefore signifies transitions in feelings and emotions. His astrological correspondence is with the mutable water sign Pisces, a sensitive, artistic sign, which is romantic and idealistic in love.

The Knight of Cups holds out a golden cup. He is young and dashing, wearing a fine, plumed cap and hunting horn – he represents a charming, idealistic person.

KNIGHT of CUPS

Interpreting the KNIGHT OF CUPS

Qualities of perfection, idealism and romance may start to colour the seeker's world, either literally through a person entering his or her life, or via the seeker's inner cultivation of these qualities. It appears that the seeker is ripe for love, and often inner readiness will manifest in a relationship. This card can also denote an interest and desire for artistic endeavours.

~ QUEEN OF CUPS ~
Beloved, adored

QUEEN OF CUPS

The Queen of Cups wears a subtly beautiful robe in the style of late-seventeenth-century Japan. She holds a red cup embossed with gold.

The Ukiyoe Tarot

The graceful Queen of Cups is associated with the 'one who is loved' or the 'adored one'. She is deeply involved with her feeling nature and, astrologically, is associated with the fixed water sign of Scorpio. She is very attuned to her ardent, passionate inner world of feelings which is of paramount importance to her. She is, therefore, fully prepared to plumb her emotional depths of either love or hate, and is loyal and generous in relationships.

Interpreting the QUEEN OF CUPS

The Queen of Cups suggests a time for inner reflection and contemplation. She may represent a person entering the seeker's life who has the capacity for profound introspection and acts as example for the seeker, or it may mean that now is the time for the seeker to be developing these qualities within himself or herself.

~ KING OF CUPS ~
Kindness, helpfulness

The Norse Tarot

The King of Cups was traditionally connected with the law or the church. In this respect he advised on the emotional, material or spiritual well-being of others but remained personally uninvolved. This is suggested in the Norse deck as he stands surrounded by water, the element of feeling, yet he is not wet. He is kind and good, yet is afraid of intimacy. Astrologically, the card is linked with Cancer, the crab – a creature belonging neither to land nor sea.

The King of Cups stands on a rock which juts out of the ocean. He holds a chalice above his head as though in an offering to the sea.

king of cups

Interpreting the KING OF CUPS

The King of Cups is the curious mixture of one who desperately wants to be involved in relationships and longs for deep intimate commitment with others, yet at the same time is frightened of such desires. When this card appears it seems to challenge the seeker to face his fears in relationships and truly examine his defences.

THE SUIT OF
~ WANDS ~

The suit of Wands is mainly associated with intuition. In medieval society Wands were linked to the peasants; and as one of the Arthurian Grail Hallows, the Wand could be seen as the lance which pierced Christ's side as He hung on the cross. In Celtic myth, the Wand may represent the spear of Lug, a skilled and multi-talented god. The Wands are also linked to the ancient element of fire, as indicated in the Haindl and Mythic decks by their torch-like appearance. They communicate the magical spark of life which represents the mysterious human ability to create images and ideas from nowhere. The fire signs in astrology have been connected with the intuitive function in Jungian psychology. The Wands in the tarot reflect extrovert and masculine qualities, representing imagination and creative energy in a reading. The Rider-Waite and Morgan-Greer decks both use wands with sprouting leaves to symbolize this creative potential.

Non-pictorial cards from the suit of Wands are shown above, belonging to the Marseilles, Swiss, Visconti, Witches, Esoteric and Ukiyoe decks (left to right).

~ ACE OF WANDS ~
A powerful rush of energy and enthusiasm

The Haindl deck gives the suit cards a direction as well as an element. The wands, which look almost spear-like, signify the East or Asia, as well as the element of fire.

Ace of Wands in the East

The Haindl Tarot

In the Haindl deck a flaming wand stands before a lingam (a phallic stone) and a yoni (a lotus flower filled with water which symbolizes female genitals). Together they reveal the male and female aspects of God combined. This produces the gift of fire, of life, of energy and optimism, traditionally associated with the Ace of Wands. The Ace is the number one, the pure energy of fire which results in an upsurge of creative energy and drive.

Interpreting the ACE OF WANDS

The Ace of Wands represents the creative life force in its purest form. Now is a time of great energy which can be put to good use in terms of laying foundations for creative ventures. It suggests that innovative ideas are in abundance and that new beginnings are imminent. There is plenty of inspiration and optimism available for dreaming up new projects.

~ TWO OF WANDS ~
Formulation of a new aim, goal or project

The Rider-Waite Tarot

This is a transition card. The pure energy of the Ace has split into opposing forces which are reflected in the image by the red roses of desire and the white lilies of the spirit. The man seems to be trying to decide on his next move, and the sprouting leaves on the wands indicate creative possibilities. This card suggests that the ideas of the Ace have been translated into action, yet there is still a long way to go before they can be fully manifest.

A man holds fast to the wand, a symbol of what he has achieved, and a globe, symbolizing future opportunities. Another wand is firmly fixed behind him.

Interpreting the TWO OF WANDS

The Two of Wands is a promising card which suggests that success is possible although it requires much commitment and hard work. The energy embodied by this card indicates the rewards for such efforts are certainly worthwhile. This card also suggests the desire for change and the wish for variety so typical of the suit of Wands.

~ THREE OF WANDS ~

Initial completion of an idea or project

A man holds two budding wands, with a third behind him. He looks out over barren plains and mountains suggesting opportunities for development.

The Morgan-Greer Tarot

The Three of Wands, the number of initial completion, suggests the fulfilment of that which was started in idea form in the Ace, set in motion in the Two and now comes to fruition. Nevertheless, it marks the initial stages of achievement only and, as indicated in the image here, there is a sense of more work and effort to come. It is a satisfying card yet the message indicates that things have to continue to move forward.

Interpreting the THREE OF WANDS

The Three of Wands is a positive card which indicates a sense of accomplishment and, consequently, satisfaction. It can also imply a certain twinge of disappointment because only the first stage is completed and there is still so much to do, but hopes are high and feelings are optimistic. The overall message is to stay on course and not lose focus.

~ FOUR OF WANDS ~

A well-earned celebration, a time of joy

The Rider-Waite Tarot

Four is a number of reality and stability. This card was traditionally associated with the rejoicing and celebration of events such as harvest festival, a time of thanksgiving and gratitude, as well as the deserved party and holiday accompanying the festivities. The image shown here effectively captures the mood of joyful merry-making. However, after the gathering of crops and the attendant sense of achievement, a return to work is inevitable.

A triumphant couple wave garlands above their heads in an expression of exultation. Four wands are festively decorated with ribbons, fruit and flowers.

Interpreting the FOUR OF WANDS

This is a pleasant card suggesting a happy time of enjoyment and leisure. It could be associated with a holiday or a time of rest and repose, or it might reflect celebrations due at the end of exams or a period of exertion. The Four of Wands indicates a time for relaxation which follows hard work, although it is clear that a return to daily routine must follow.

‒ FIVE OF WANDS ‒

Struggles in life, petty irritations and short-term difficulties

FIVE OF WANDS

Jason confronts reality, in the shape of the dragon, in order to realize his dreams, in the Golden Fleece. The torch-like wands symbolize fiery energy.

The Mythic Tarot

The Five, the number of uncertainty and change, indicates a period of frustration in the suit of Wands, when everything seems difficult and nothing goes according to plan. The Mythic Tarot uses the story of Jason and the Golden Fleece to illustrate the divinatory meanings of this suit. Here Jason's challenging struggle to obtain the Fleece from the clutches of the dragon is depicted – a symbol of the struggle between desire and reality.

Interpreting the FIVE OF WANDS

This card suggests a time in which everyday life gets very hectic and all manner of things feel particularly irritating and trying. None of these obstacles is insurmountable yet they are annoying and frustrating. The Five of Wands symbolizes the difficulties that can arise when trying to translate ideas into the real or material world.

‒ SIX OF WANDS ‒

Victory, success and public acclaim

The Russian Tarot of St Petersburg

Six, a number composed of two triangles, represents equilibrium and harmony. In the suit of Wands, it is the card of victory and achievement in the world. The conquering champion clearly denotes a proud sense of accomplishment and triumph which follows the effort and discipline needed to bring a task to fruition. The kind of recognition that is received with this card is very public and opens the seeker to society's praise or, indeed, its criticism.

The champion, crowned with a laurel wreath and brandishing a shining wand, leads a procession of soldiers carrying his train and waving a banner.

Six of Clubs

Interpreting the SIX OF WANDS

The Six of Wands is an optimistic card. In terms of progress and acclaim by society's standards, it is very positive, implying success and recognition for achievement. It can also denote work promotion and good career prospects. This card brings with it promise of fulfilment and satisfaction in working and public life.

~ SEVEN OF WANDS ~

Stiff competition in work and career

A determined-looking man pushes back sturdy wands that block his way. He is dressed for cold weather which may signify the chill winds of rivalry.

The Morgan-Greer Tarot

Seven is the number of wisdom and knowledge. The Morgan-Greer deck depicts the Seven of Wands as a man battling against six wands which rise up against him. After the victory and success of the Six of Wands is the increased competition which inevitably comes hot on the heels of any kind of promotion. Reaching a peak of success is the first task, but holding on to it and improving on it is the next and often more difficult phase.

Interpreting the SEVEN OF WANDS

This challenging card suggests the need to keep moving, learning and enhancing skills and talents. It points to competition, which can be healthy as it spurs one on to further heights, and it implies progression in career – but success will be hard won. The Seven of Wands can also suggest teaching, writing and lecturing.

~ EIGHT OF WANDS ~

A time of activity and excitement

The Norse Tarot

The number Eight denotes regeneration and change. The image on the Norse deck shows cooperation between the oarsmen as their oars, representing the eight wands, move together through the water. The prevailing circumstances seem to be helpful, in that the sea is peaceful and the sun shines down on their vessel. This is a card of energy and action. The fiery enthusiasm of the wands is coupled with friendly external forces which go to create an atmosphere of excitement.

Eight men row a vessel speedily through calm seas. It seems that progress is smooth and steady and that the destination is within easy reach.

Interpreting the EIGHT OF WANDS

The Eight of Wands suggests a time for action, not thought. Planning stages and delays are over and it is time to put ideas in motion now that creative energy can be put to good use. A busy but happy time lies ahead which is likely to include travel.

~ NINE OF WANDS ~

Strength in reserve, a spurt of energy

Nine of Clubs

A soldier battles his way through a thick wood. He clears his path with down-turned wands – one remains upright, a symbol of his last vestige of strength.

The Russian Tarot of St Petersburg

The Nine is the number in which all others are summed up to form a foundation before the final completion in the Ten. The Nine of Wands indicates a position of strength even in the face of considerable adversity. Determination is needed to face the trials ahead. As the man depicted on the Russian deck struggles through the wood, we see the significant difficulties he has to negotiate; yet despite this opposition, he battles on resolutely.

Interpreting the NINE OF WANDS

The Nine of Wands denotes a reserve of strength. So, even when events seem overwhelming and the odds look very shaky, there is just enough stamina and might to push through to the finish line. This card offers courage and determination to overcome obstacles and achieve goals in spite of difficult circumstances.

~ TEN OF WANDS ~

Heavy burdens, the need to learn limits

The Mythic Tarot

Here we rejoin the myth of Jason: he has captured the Golden Fleece, become king and had children with Medea; yet still he feels dissatisfied. Thinking another kingdom and crown will help, he pursues the Princess of Corinth for a wife. This enrages Medea, who kills their children and his newly betrothed, leaving Jason lonely, bereft and suicidal. Before he can hang himself, a piece of the Argos, his ship which now lies rotting, falls and crushes him to death.

Jason is crushed by the flaming wands of his own desires. He has taken on too much and ultimately destroys all the good he worked so hard for.

TEN OF WANDS

Interpreting the TEN OF WANDS

The Ten of Wands reveals the dangers of this suit, warning against a tendency to become overburdened. The fiery element of the Wands is filled with imagination, often travelling beyond the realm of the earthly plane. Consequently it is often disappointed by physical restrictions. This card spells out the pitfalls of taking on too much or ignoring limits.

~ PAGE OF WANDS ~

Inspirations, seeds of new beginnings in creativity

VALET·DE·BATON

A young man dressed as a messenger holds forward the wand of creative ideas. His youth is a symbol of potential unfulfilled.

Le Tarot de Marseilles

The Page of Wands is a fiery card showing a young man to represent the opportunities and possibilities that youth always offers. The Pages are messengers and, in the case of the suit of Wands, the Page carries news of a creative variety, as he brings ideas of an imaginative nature to the seeker. He represents the fragile new beginnings of a creative process which will need much careful nurturing if it is to be brought to fruition.

Interpreting the PAGE OF WANDS

The Page of Wands usually represents the budding of new ideas, often of a creative or artistic nature. These are accompanied by the gradual growth of enthusiasm and faith in them required to bring them to maturity. Anything young and small needs lots of assistance in the early stages to help it reach its full potential.

~ KNIGHT OF WANDS ~

Change of residence, journeys, moves

The Ukiyoe Tarot

The Knight of Wands in the Ukiyoe deck represents a seeker of inner rather than outer truth. The Knights in the tarot seem to link with the mutable signs in astrology, which would connect the Knight of Wands with Sagittarius, the restless, enthusiastic fire sign which is always searching for new ways. Sagittarius is the archetypal traveller and the Knight of Wands is traditionally associated with changes: of residence, of job and even of country.

A pilgrim with no possessions other than his horse and armed only with a wand rides towards the mountains seeking spiritual rather than physical combat.

KNIGHT OF WANDS

Interpreting the KNIGHT OF WANDS

The Knight of Wands can be literally interpreted as a move of house or home. However, there is more to the card than just that. There also is a strong impulse to discover, to learn and to know about things beyond an everyday level, matters of philosophical or spiritual interest. The seeker may be filled with powerful creative and artistic desires or drives.

~ QUEEN OF WANDS ~
Hearth and home

The Queen of Wands is shown here as a mature woman with long brown hair holding a sturdy wand of rulership and strength.

The Swiss 1JJ Tarot

The Queen of Wands is an energetic and capable woman, sometimes linked with Leo, the element of fixed fire. The 'fixed' quality combines with fire to produce creative energy which is firmly contained and therefore very productive. Traditionally this card is known as 'queen of hearth and home', yet she is also creative, talented and strong-willed. Her rule over the domestic domain is coupled with keen pursuits of other areas of interest.

Interpreting the QUEEN OF WANDS

The Queen of Wands symbolizes the development of the qualities of loyalty, steadfastness, industry and creative talents, either in the seeker or through someone entering the seeker's life. She may represent a person who is full of warmth and compassion, yet is strong, independent and positive. She makes a good and generous friend or a formidable foe.

~ KING OF WANDS ~
Warmth, enthusiasm and confidence

The Mythic Tarot

The King of Wands is connected in the Mythic Tarot with Theseus of Athens, whose bravery helped rid the Cretan King Minos of the dreadful Minotaur. This card is connected with the sign of Aries, and Theseus embodies the qualities of this vibrant sign – he is brave, sometimes foolhardy, charming and persuasive, with a flair for pulling off the difficult and a strong talent for inspiring those around him to attempt the impossible.

A king dressed in red robes holds a flaming wand. His throne is carved with rams' heads, and behind him stands a ram, symbol of Aries, the cardinal fiery sign.

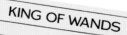

KING OF WANDS

Interpreting the KING OF WANDS

The King of Wands suggests that the qualities of imagination, energy and zest for life are to enter the seeker's life either through an inner quest, or through someone entering his or her life. The King is fun and generous with a good sense of humour. He is an optimistic visionary and life is seldom dull when his influence is strong – neither is it peaceful!

THE SUIT OF
~ SWORDS ~

The Swords are connected with the intellect and thought process. If the suits are linked to social divisions, the Swords are associated with nobility. And, if we use the Grail Hallows as a category, the Swords might be linked with the Old Testament as King David's Sword of the Spirit. This suit could also be connected with Celtic myth as the Sword of Nuada, king of the gods, whose Sword was so powerful that no enemy could ever hope to escape it once it was unsheathed. Air is the element of the Swords – the breath of life – and the air signs in astrology can be associated with the thinking function in Jungian psychology. Although the Swords are traditionally linked with difficulties and sorrow, they can also signify the capacity for reflection and understanding.

Non-pictorial cards from the suit of Swords are shown above, belonging to the Marseilles, Swiss, Visconti, Witches, Esoteric and Ukiyoe decks (left to right).

~ ACE OF SWORDS ~

The double-edged Sword that cuts for good and ill

The olive branch of peace and the palm of victory emerge from the golden crown suggesting attainment. The red and white roses stand for spirit and matter.

The Morgan-Greer Tarot

The Aces mark new beginnings and the Ace of Swords, the suit of difficulty and strife, is a double-edged sword which can cut two ways – for the good of humankind and for its detriment. The element of air linked to this suit is ambivalent as it symbolizes the uniquely human capacity to formulate ideas and think logically and conceptually. This can produce, on the one hand, the advancement of medicine, yet, on the other, an atomic bomb.

Interpreting the ACE OF SWORDS

The Ace of Swords suggests that a new beginning, which may not look initially promising, can reach a satisfactory conclusion. It denotes strength and courage even in troublesome situations and ultimately indicates the promise of good overcoming evil. Conflict is often necessary to force change and usually encourages the search for new, positive solutions.

~ TWO OF SWORDS ~

A stalemate, indecision, refusal to make a choice

The Rider-Waite Tarot

The Two of Swords represents a state of paralysis or stalemate which prevents any action from taking place. The Rider-Waite deck uses an image of a blindfolded woman which indicates that she refuses to look at her circumstances, and ignores her emotions and the facts of the matter. Instead she simply sits tight, keeping the two swords she is holding in perfect balance, thus maintaining the equilibrium.

The blindfolded woman on this card ignores the sea of emotion which lies behind her and the rocks of hard fact which jut from it.

Interpreting the TWO OF SWORDS

The Two of Swords in a reading suggests an impasse, a situation which is not satisfactory yet there is a great reluctance to upset the prevailing balance. The conflict usually reflected in the Twos is suppressed and a stalemate results. However, it is clear that the tension in this card will have to be addressed sooner or later.

⁓ THREE OF SWORDS ⁓
The darkest hour comes just before the dawn

A bleeding heart, pierced with swords, indicates sorrow. However, light is breaking through the dark clouds bringing peace after the storm.

The Morgan-Greer Tarot

After the strife of the Ace followed by the tension of the Two, the Three – being the number of initial completion – signals the situation coming to a head. While the image is unpleasant, the light encircling the heart suggests that a necessary clearing has taken place and that insight and understanding can help mend the wound. This card indicates a sense of relief that the poison is no longer beneath the surface so that healing can now begin.

Interpreting the THREE OF SWORDS

Although the picture the Three of Swords paints is not a very cheerful one, it nevertheless indicates that a time for clearing away old conflicts is necessary and healthy in order to develop and encourage new ways. It offers a sense of perspective and vision which can put a positive light on dark and difficult times – 'the darkest hour comes just before the dawn'.

⁓ FOUR OF SWORDS ⁓
Rest and retreat after activity, convalescence

The Russian Tarot of St Petersburg

The Four of Swords is a card of repose and calm. It indicates a time for necessary withdrawal from the hurly-burly of daily life. The sleeping figure in the Russian deck looks peaceful and the swords barring the closed window suggest that the time for fighting is over. This is a card of tranquillity and recuperation after struggles or battles. The message of this card is perhaps especially important in the modern world of stress and anxiety.

A sleeping man, maybe a soldier, rests beneath an open window. The church spires in the distance may represent his need to concentrate on his spiritual life.

Four of Swords

Interpreting the FOUR OF SWORDS

The Four of Swords suggests the need for convalescence or rest after a period of great energy or conflict. A quiet time of calm contemplation is necessary after hard work or a particularly demanding time. The natural cycles of activity and periods of calm are reflected in this card, this period being one of quietude and relaxation.

~ FIVE OF SWORDS ~

Acceptance of limitations, a need to work within boundaries

FIVE OF SWORDS

Apollo tells Orestes how his mother has murdered his father. He hands the swords to the youth demanding that he kill his mother to avenge his father's death.

The Mythic Tarot

The Five of Swords indicates the need to acknowledge limitations and work within the confines of the reality of one's situation. The Mythic Tarot describes the struggle of Orestes to work with his inherited family squabbles, none of which are actually his fault, yet he has to deal with the predicament because he belongs to that family. It is not fair, certainly, but it is how it is and he must work with those shortcomings as creatively as possible.

Interpreting the FIVE OF SWORDS

The Five of Swords is a card in which the seeker must realistically face his or her position and act in a way most constructive to that situation, rather than blindly attempting to force through a result which is clearly not going to work. It is a time when limitations and blocks need to be accepted before changes can take place.

~ SIX OF SWORDS ~

Moving away from turbulence towards calmer times

The Rider-Waite Tarot

The Six, the number of harmony, brings a sense of peace to the normally uncomfortable Swords. The image suggests a moving away from troubled times towards happier calmer times ahead. The movement from strife indicates the resolution of the Five in the Six. Accepting the confines of one's situation can be the first step to understanding it, which, in turn, helps contain the difficulties and represents a positive use of the thinking function.

A ferryman rows two figures to a distant shore. The water on the right of the boat is rough, while they are moving towards calmer waters on the left.

Interpreting the SIX OF SWORDS

The Six of Swords means moving away from anxious times towards something more contented. It can indicate a literal move in terms of a change of environment, residence or country, or it can suggest that the journey is an inner one, moving away from destructive or negative patterns of thinking and seeking more optimism and hope.

~ SEVEN OF SWORDS ~
A need for diplomacy or tact

A sleeping dragon protects a hoard of gold while a man creeps stealthily away, trying not to wake the beast.

The Norse Tarot

The Norse deck uses an image which implies stealth and cunning, as the man makes a careful escape from the dragon's lair. The Seven of Swords is connected with the need to use evasion or diplomacy in a situation, rather than direct confrontation. The thinking function is essential here in terms of planning and strategy which might be necessary to produce the best results, even though one's tactics may be somewhat questionable.

Interpreting the SEVEN OF SWORDS

The Seven of Swords implies that a situation in the seeker's life requires that he or she apply mental energy in a prudent way. This card signifies that the time is not right for aggressive or confrontational stances; instead tact, diplomacy and even subterfuge may be necessary – it would not be wise to show an opponent your hand in poker.

~ EIGHT OF SWORDS ~
Fear of moving out of a situation of restriction

The Mythic Tarot

The Eight of Swords depicts a difficult choice. It seems as though no matter which decision one makes there are major disadvantages attached. In the Mythic deck, Orestes is torn between the law of Apollo who will torment him if he does not avenge his father's death, and, as this involves matricide, the Furies, who will punish him if he does. Obviously, our choices are not normally this drastic, but the card does reflect an unhappy dilemma.

Orestes is trapped between the sun god Apollo, who demands that he kill his own mother, and the horrific goddesses of vengeance, the Furies.

EIGHT OF SWORDS

Interpreting the EIGHT OF SWORDS

The Eight of Swords suggests a situation in which the seeker feels stuck. He or she may be facing a difficult choice or be perhaps feeling afraid of moving out of an unhappy or restrictive situation, even though it may be in his or her power to do so. On a positive note, this card predicts that a sign will come to show a way out.

~ NINE OF SWORDS ~

A vision of impending doom which may not be the reality

A woman weeps as nine swords point menacingly down at her – although they do not touch her. The candles burn softly while outside the sky is dark.

The Russian Tarot of St Petersburg

The Nine of Swords signifies a sense of disaster or dread which is more in the mind than in actuality. The dark image which the Russian deck depicts clearly suggests distress, yet the woman is apparently unharmed and the grief seems to come from within rather than without. The picture conjures up fears and anxieties. It is traditionally known as the card of nightmares, which, though they may be terrifying, are not real.

Interpreting the NINE OF SWORDS

The Nine of Swords suggests that the seeker may be overwhelmed by inner doubts or fears that may not translate into anything actual in the material world. The torment and affliction seem to be in the seeker's mind and, although very distressing, there is nothing external to fear. The inner worries do, however, need to be taken seriously and understood.

~ TEN OF SWORDS ~

An ending which is inevitable, yet promises new beginnings

The Morgan-Greer Tarot

The Ten of Swords is a card of endings. There is no doubt from the image on this deck that something is over: the swords have pierced the man's body and he is clearly dead. However, the glimmer of hope in the sky – the light rising in the distance – suggests that a new beginning is already in sight. Endings are not necessarily bad: they are rather part of life's cycle of birth, blossom, fruit and decay, and nothing ends that has not been fully lived out.

A figure lies face down in the snow with ten swords piercing his back. A thin strip of blue sky emerging out of the darkness indicates promise for the future.

Interpreting the TEN OF SWORDS

The Ten of Swords obviously indicates that something is ending. What exactly that is cannot be gleaned from the card. It may concern the ending of a partnership or relationship, a child leaving home, the ending of a job, or moving house – it is an open question. However, whenever something ends, something new is waiting to begin.

~ PAGE OF SWORDS ~

Intelligence, youthfulness and an inclination to gossip

The Page of Swords represents someone who has potential for innovative thinking. He stands on a chequer board, which may symbolize the game of life in its sharp contrasts.

El Gran Tarot Esoterico

The Pages all represent the start of something new and the imagery here uses a young man embarking on a journey to denote a new beginning. The youth bears a sword, carefully sheathed away, signifying inner knowledge. He looks to the horizon, symbolizing vision and the ability to notice what others do not see. The Page of Swords is the messenger of the element of air, indicating a stirring in the intellect of new ideas and ways of thinking.

Interpreting the PAGE OF SWORDS

The Page of Swords, like all the Pages, is usually connected with someone or something in its embryonic form. The Pages suggest small beginnings and the Page of Swords represents potential in the realm of thinking. At best, he indicates a clear, original thinker and, at worst, a gossip, or one who spreads rumours.

~ KNIGHT OF SWORDS ~

Excitement, ambition and upheaval

Cary-Yale Visconti Tarocchi

This card traditionally signifies an attractive, rather fascinating person who enters the seeker's life suddenly and changes it drastically – often bringing a certain amount of chaos with him or her. The Knights of the tarot are all seekers, and, as the Knight of Swords reflects the element of air and Gemini in astrology, he therefore seeks mental stimulation and knowledge. He enjoys both imparting and receiving information.

A young man in armour carries a double-edged sword with apparent confidence, as though he is unperturbed by the conflict of battle ahead.

Interpreting the KNIGHT OF SWORDS

When the Knight of Swords appears in a layout he heralds changes in the seeker's life. He may represent an actual person who has the qualities of air – talkative, active, with a keen mind and a nerve of steel – who literally changes the seeker's life, or he may reflect those qualities being developed within the seeker, perhaps through study or work.

~ QUEEN OF SWORDS ~

Strength, determination, courage in adversity

QUEEN of SWORDS.

The Queen wears a cloak patterned with clouds and sits on a throne carved with birds, butterflies and angels, linking her to the element of air.

The Rider-Waite Tarot

The Queen of Swords is traditionally associated with a sense of sorrow or disappointment; this image is one of stoic suffering. The Queen sits alone, proud and erect, her face set in an expression of grim determination, apparently ignoring the storm clouds gathering in the distance. She represents one who has suffered or lost, yet bears the pain bravely and without fuss. Astrologically, this card is linked to the fixed air sign Aquarius.

Interpreting the QUEEN OF SWORDS

The Queen of Swords suggests one who knows what it means to be alone and to face adversity. The seeker may need to learn to bear his or her difficulties without complaint and draw strength from knowledge and experience. Anxieties need to be contained with patience and courage until circumstances become more favourable.

~ KING OF SWORDS ~

Sternness and severity combined with justice and compassion

The Swiss 1JJ Tarot

The King of Swords is traditionally connected with nobility and was thought to represent an authority figure with a keen regard for truth and justice. He is associated with the legal profession for his capacity for clear impartial reasoning which he uses to judge and decide dispassionately what the fairest solution to any problem might be. Astrologically he seems to describe Libra, the air sign, which is closely connected with equality and balance.

The King of Swords is depicted as a powerful monarch dressed in full armour with a crown upon his helmet, and his sword pointing up as a symbol of righteousness.

Interpreting the KING OF SWORDS

The King of Swords signifies either that someone who has strong convictions and a firm moral code will become a part of the seeker's life, or that the seeker will be searching for such qualities within himself or herself. The King of Swords is honourable and just, always wanting to seek out that which is fair and equal in life.

KING of SWORDS

THE SUIT OF
~ PENTACLES ~

The Pentacles, or Coins, are associated primarily with the material world. In medieval society they were connected to the merchants. They are also linked with the Platter found in the Arthurian Grail castle from which Jesus and his followers ate at the Last Supper. The Cups, Swords, Wands and Pentacles are also found in earlier Celtic myth: the Pentacle being associated by some with the Stone of Fal, the coronation seat of Irish kings, or the Stone of Saint Columba which was thought to be able to float magically. The Pentacles can also be connected with the the oldest element of all, earth. The earth signs in astrology are linked with the sensation function in Jungian psychology. In the tarot, the Pentacles represent the senses, the body and the relationship to the material world.

Non-pictorial cards from the suit of Pentacles are shown above, belonging to the Marseilles, Swiss, Visconti, Witches, Esoteric and Ukiyoe decks (left to right).

~ ACE OF PENTACLES ~
Good beginnings for financial propositions

The Haindl Tarot

This card is called the Ace of Stones in the West, which represents North America. Here an eagle lands on the Stone while a rainbow shines overhead.

The Ace of Pentacles depicts the meeting of earth and sky, feminine and masculine, reality and spirit, represented respectively in the Haindl Tarot by the stone and eagle. The rainbow, the bird and the rock all symbolize the gifts of the earth, and this suit is concerned with the element of earth, the body and the sensation function. The Ace suggests new beginnings in the material realm, perhaps in the form of worldly status or financial gain.

Interpreting the ACE OF PENTACLES

The Ace of Pentacles indicates healthy prospects for financial and business ventures. It can suggest the founding of business enterprises or funding new projects. It reflects the birth of something new in material form – seeds may be sown in the form of taking a new job, setting up a home or creating a business.

Ace of Stones in the West

~ TWO OF PENTACLES ~
Change or fluctuation in fortunes, yet harmony within change

The Mythic Tarot

The myth of Daedalus, master craftsman of Athens, is the Mythic Tarot's storyline for the earthy suit of Pentacles. The Two is the number of growth, of translating the ideas of the Ace into the first stages of concrete reality. Daedalus is taking the first steps towards becoming a seriously recognized artist. Two golden pentacles support his wooden table, on which lie his first attempts at creating the intricate works of art which later made him so famous.

Daedalus, setting up his workshop, proudly holds up two of his early inventions, the saw and the axe. Vines appear throughout this suit as a symbol of the earth's riches.

TWO OF PENTACLES

Interpreting the TWO OF PENTACLES

The Two of Pentacles shows a time of movement and a need to operate with the shifting energy which is at work when a new venture is being established. In the early stages, much experimentation is necessary and this card denotes a need to skilfully juggle the various factors involved in order for the enterprise to succeed.

~ THREE OF PENTACLES ~

A first structure is created yet there is much work ahead

An artisan is hard at work on a church or cathedral. The shell of the building is clearly in place, yet there is still much to be achieved.

The Morgan-Greer Tarot

The Morgan-Greer deck has used the theme of the craftsman or designer working on the details of a building. As well as initial completion, the Three is the number of growth and expansion; and the image here depicts the continuation of work required for a design to be truly fulfilled. In many ways, getting a project done in outline is quite easy – the difficult part is keeping up the momentum to finish it off to a high standard.

Interpreting the THREE OF PENTACLES

The Three of Pentacles represents a sense of satisfaction when the first stages of an endeavour have been realized. The outline is complete but there is still much to do. Like all the Threes, while there is a justifiable cause for satisfaction, this is only the beginning and sustained effort is essential in order to reach a pleasing result.

~ FOUR OF PENTACLES ~

If nothing is risked, nothing can be gained

The Rider-Waite Tarot

The Four of Pentacles has been called 'the card of the miser', the one who will not let go of a penny and jealously guards his possessions. Generally, a miser will grow increasingly paranoid and suspicious of other people's motives and finds it difficult to form good relationships as a consequence. The sense of nothing, either financial or emotional, being open or shared results in the person becoming increasingly stuck, as suggested in this image.

A man holds on tightly to all he has achieved. He grasps one pentacle close to his chest and keeps his feet firmly on two more, while the fourth sits on top of his crown.

Interpreting the FOUR OF PENTACLES

The Four of Pentacles suggests the dangers involved in not taking risks and not having sufficient faith in the unknown; for only when the seeker is open to giving can he or she hope to receive. Money can also be equated with emotions, so miserliness can be extended to emotional restraint. The fear involved in letting go must be confronted.

~ FIVE OF PENTACLES ~

Financial, emotional or spiritual loss

A couple struggle through a thick snowstorm. The woman tries to protect her child under her cloak, implying inner feelings of fear and doubt.

The Norse Tarot

The Five of Pentacles, like all the Fives, carries a sense of uncertainty and anxiety. The couple shown on the Norse deck are clearly apprehensive. In fact they seem so concerned with their predicament that they may fail to notice the five pentacles half buried in the snow. The sense of loss that is linked with this card could be financial loss or money worries; yet on a deeper level it could suggest a loss of faith.

Interpreting the FIVE OF PENTACLES

The Five of Pentacles is traditionally linked with financial or material difficulties; yet there is an undertone which suggests that it may be hard to hold on to a sense of meaning and purpose in life. This card offers a warning to the seeker to be attentive in all areas, emotional, financial or spiritual, for fear of losing sight of what is truly important.

~ SIX OF PENTACLES ~

Generosity, benevolence and kindness

The Russian Tarot of St Petersburg

The Russian deck uses the image of alms being given to the poor to reflect the message of harmony and balance that the Six brings to the suit of Pentacles. It communicates the need for a balance in wealth and power for harmony to exist. Generosity can take the form of material aid or it can be help of an emotional nature. Wealth is about far more than money: it means spiritual and emotional riches as well.

A wealthy knight or lord gives gold to an obviously poorer man. Riches, whether material, emotional or spiritual, can be profitably shared among men.

Six of Coins

Interpreting the SIX OF PENTACLES

The Six of Pentacles reminds us that it is the kindness and generosity of friends that makes life feel good. Friends in need are aided – whether the seeker is helped by the benevolence of his or her friends, or he or she must supply that benefit to others. The Six is the number of goodwill, and in the suit of Pentacles it describes practical aid and assistance.

~ SEVEN OF PENTACLES ~

A choice to be made, difficult decisions to be taken

A farmer faces a crop of five pentacles, while his hoe points to two behind him, symbolizing a possible choice between the secure and the more adventurous.

The Morgan-Greer Tarot

The Seven of Pentacles symbolizes a pause in the development of an idea or creative work. Seven is the number of wisdom and can be connected with the world's creation – six days of labour and the seventh day of rest. In the Morgan-Greer deck, we see the fruits of the farmer's labours in the form of the five pentacles on the left; yet a further vision of two pentacles seems to be emerging on the right, which might signal changes in the existing order.

Interpreting the SEVEN OF PENTACLES

The Seven of Pentacles suggests that a crossroads has been reached in terms of deciding whether to keep on with something that has been established and is working well, or whether to risk changes which might threaten the status quo. The card does not indicate which direction the seeker should take, only that a choice will emerge and will need to be considered.

~ EIGHT OF PENTACLES ~

The apprentice, the enthusiastic student

The Rider-Waite Tarot

As the number of regeneration and rebirth, the Eight of Pentacles signifies an apprentice, or mature student, one who wants to commit himself or herself to a new form of study or skill. It may symbolize a person who changes career quite late in life, as it is not the card of a school leaver, but rather of someone who realizes their direction needs to change and is prepared to work hard to ensure that the next move is a positive one.

A cheerful-looking man is energetically carving pentacles. His past efforts are displayed on the post beside him as he works on the task in hand.

Interpreting the EIGHT OF PENTACLES

The Eight of Pentacles suggests that it is a good time for studying, learning and for turning skills or talents into money-making ventures. It indicates that hard work can translate into a practical application of ideas. This, in turn, can form the foundation for a profitable venture, both financially and creatively rewarding.

⁓ NINE OF PENTACLES ⁓

Pleasure and comfort through material success and achievement

A woman wears a rich fur-trimmed cloak decorated with golden pentacles, a symbol of wealth. A casket full of gold sits in the sand at her feet.

The Norse Tarot

The Pentacles are earthy so they often relate to physical attainment, and the Nine of Pentacles in the Norse deck shows an image of satisfaction after much effort and labour. It suggests that the seeker is able to fully enjoy the sense of gratification that his or her hard work has achieved. Although this card does not necessarily indicate that the seeker will be alone, it does carry with it a sense of being content to enjoy one's own company.

Interpreting the NINE OF PENTACLES

The Nine of Pentacles symbolizes comfort on a number of levels: physical, financial and emotional. The seeker may experience a sense of very basic pleasure in the knowledge that what he or she has achieved is good. This card indicates a high level of personal self-esteem which is enduring and most satisfying.

⁓ TEN OF PENTACLES ⁓

Foundations for families, fortunes or lasting traditions

The Mythic Tarot

The Ten is the number of completion. The cycle of the earthy Pentacles is concerned with creating something physical or tangible which will last longer than one human lifetime and will make that one life meaningful. This can be achieved through children continuing the bloodline, or through works of art, books, inventions or ideas which are made concrete in some way so that they continue to exist long after their creator has ceased to.

The last instalment in the life of Daedalus shows him as an old man who has finally fulfilled his dreams, as his children and grandchildren enjoy his creations.

TEN OF PENTACLES

Interpreting the TEN OF PENTACLES

The Ten of Pentacles signifies a desire to put down roots. It may be in terms of starting a family, buying a home, purchasing something as a family heirloom, or founding a tradition. It suggests, in fact, doing anything which adds a sense of permanence and stability to life. The urge to create something lasting is very strong.

～ PAGE OF PENTACLES ～

A respect for the material side of life

A samurai's servant is in the foothills of the mountains to signify a journey. While the samurai is above interest in material matters, his servant must attend to them.

The Ukiyoe Tarot

The Page of Pentacles represents the early stages of the process by which ideas are formed and made manifest in the material world. The element of earth represents a slow but sure process of maturation which cannot be hurried, and its fruits can only be ripened and enjoyed if the early stages are carefully nurtured and protected. Although this process is gradual and no short cuts can be taken, the end results are ultimately satisfying.

Interpreting the PAGE OF PENTACLES

The Page of Pentacles represents beginnings which, although small, are significant and must be taken seriously for the seed to germinate. It can suggest that hobbies may gradually translate into a means of making an income, or that there is an opportunity to start a career which shows promise, albeit from the bottom rung of the ladder.

～ KNIGHT OF PENTACLES ～

Hard work and attention to detail

The Norse Tarot

The Knight of Pentacles – called the Princess of Discs here – is linked to the earth sign Virgo. Qualities commonly attributed to this sign are industry, diligence and fastidious attention to detail. This is a person who works well behind the scenes to ensure everything is in its proper place, making a success out of what they do. They will be dependable and serious and will carry out any task they undertake to its satisfactory completion.

The Princess – corresponding to the Knight card – thoughtfully contemplates a large disc, indicating an ability to concentrate.

Interpreting the KNIGHT OF PENTACLES

This card suggests a need to develop the attribute of perseverance and the capacity for industry. The seeker may meet someone who has these qualities or they may be trying to find them within. The Knight of Pentacles signifies the importance of earthy values and the need for slow progress even though it may seem unglamorous.

~ QUEEN OF PENTACLES ~
Wealth and generosity

The Tarot of the Witches

A woman, crowned with gold, holds aloft a pentacle, or coin. She is dressed in green, the colour of earth, the element of the Pentacles.

The Queen of Pentacles, or Coins as they are called here, can be linked with the astrological sign of Taurus, the fixed earth sign of the bull. She is traditionally associated with a woman of material means who enjoys such things as fine clothes, good food and comfortable surroundings, and is prepared to work hard to achieve such luxuries. The earth signs all signify this commitment to hard work in order to gain rewards, and the Queen is no exception.

QUEEN OF COINS

Interpreting the QUEEN OF PENTACLES

The Queen of Pentacles suggests that a person who displays earthy qualities may enter the seeker's life, or that the seeker needs to pay attention to material demands from within. It may also imply that the seeker needs to take physical care of his or her body, or perhaps needs to be particularly alert to health matters, diet and exercise.

~ KING OF PENTACLES ~
Position and wealth, hard work

El Gran Tarot Esoterico

The King of Pentacles is often associated with Capricorn, the goat, the sign linked with ambition to achieve authority, status and financial success. He is reminiscent of the mountain goat in that he is prepared to climb high up the mountain, so determined is he to reach the highest point, his chosen goal. Perseverance and determination are key words for this card as well as the necessary courage to keep going across the roughest terrain.

The King of Pentacles is seated on a green throne with a symbol of Capricorn engraved on either side. He holds a golden rod of authority and a pile of coins.

Interpreting the KING OF PENTACLES

Like the Queen, the King of Pentacles indicates the positive energy which is needed in order to make a success of things both materially and in terms of position and status. A person may enter the seeker's life who spurs him or her on to achieve more, or the seeker may be wanting to develop that side within.

CHAPTER FOUR

READING THE CARDS

Now you are familiar with the cards of the Major and Minor Arcana, you will be ready to put what you have learned into practice. Some of you will want to know how to read the tarot for yourselves and some will wish to read for others. Many of you will want to do both!

As you turn to consult the cards it is worth reflecting for a moment on this urge to find some sort of meaning in life which may have led you to the tarot. This existential quest seems to be unique to humankind; as far as we know, animals are not bothered by such questions. They do not wonder why they exist or what life is all about; they just try to find the most secure and comfortable existence possible, and survive in it. Human beings do, however, seem to be universally vexed by impossible questions: why are we here, what is the purpose of life, is there a purpose, is there a supreme being and if so what does It want from us?

Religions and philosophies address these questions which continue to puzzle and fascinate us as they have done since the beginning of time. The tarot may also have originated as a means by which man tried to understand what the gods wanted from him, in the same way that studying the stars and their movements has, from ancient times, been an attempt to make some order and sense out of our universe.

BEFORE YOU BEGIN

Before we tackle the subject of reading the cards, it is always worth considering what can and cannot be gained from consulting the tarot. When someone approaches a tarot reader there may be a subtle search for meaning behind the stated question of 'Should I move job?' or 'Will I get married?' or any of those sorts of questions which are regularly asked. Most people come for readings to seek a sort of guidance, clarity or reassurance about their lives. Of course, some people may come with unreasonable expectations, wishing, or even expecting, the reader to use the cards to solve all their problems and make decisions for them! While we know that this is not realistic, it is possible to get drawn into thinking that we ought to be able to do this and feel as though we have 'failed' if we cannot. I therefore believe that it is extremely important to think carefully about these issues and find your own position on them, particularly if you are planning to read the tarot for another person.

In my view, a tarot reading, whether the cards are being spread for yourself or for another, ought to be a helpful and therapeutic experience. When doing a reading for yourself, you should have an aim in mind: what are you addressing the cards for? Why do you feel the need to consult them? When doing a reading for someone else, it is important to create a space in which the seeker can feel heard, as well as be given an opportunity to look from a different perspective at the point that he or she has arrived at in life.

The aim of a tarot reading, I believe, is to empower the seeker to make choices that he or she can feel content with, rather than to make wild predictions or dramatic statements. I have heard too many 'horror stories' about the effect that ill-chosen words can have when delivered through the 'authority' of a tarot reader. It is, therefore, extremely important to think carefully about *what* you say to the seeker and *how* you say it.

For example, a young woman consulted me after she had seen a card reader who had told her that she would marry a man who would die; and later she would marry another man with whom she would find happiness. Although she protested that she did not *really* believe it, the young woman was nevertheless distressed, and deep-down inside felt that she should never marry anyone as it would 'make me a sort of murderer', she told me. My personal feeling is that there is no justification at all for making a statement of this nature. How this prediction was arrived at in any case is certainly questionable, but, as card readers, we do need to be very aware of the impact we may have on people. My own position is to avoid making 'predictions' of any kind, preferring to allow the images on cards to reflect the influences that are currently available in the seeker's life and to encourage the seeker to use that information in making personal choices.

Preparing for a Reading

When preparing to do a reading for yourself or someone else it is important to find a quiet place where you will not be interrupted by external distractions like other people coming in and out or the telephone ringing. It is necessary to create a safe comfortable atmosphere in which to work and to take that work seriously; so I would not advise doing readings at parties or in public places or with other people watching. Some readers like to burn aromatherapy oils which are conducive to relaxation, while others like to burn scented candles or incense. My preparation is to take a few quiet minutes to clear my mind before starting a reading, doing some breathing exercises and generally relaxing. I repeat this exercise at the end of each session too.

Setting aside a certain amount of time for a session is also important, as a reading that goes on much beyond an hour and a half is likely to get very tiring for both the reader and the seeker. I feel it is preferable to stop at a set time, if necessary setting another time to continue if it does not feel finished. This is better than going on for hours at a time which ends up being emotionally and mentally draining for both parties.

I usually make a tape recording of the session so that the seeker may take away a record of the reading to reflect on in his or her own time. I would also advise that you make a second copy for yourself so that you can monitor your own progress as a reader – listening to a reading you have given can be very useful as a form of personal supervision.

Laying out the Cards

For a reading, I lay out the cards on a square of black silk, and then use this cloth to wrap around the cards when not in use. This ritual follows old traditions in which black silk was thought to act as an insulator from negative vibrations. Laying the cards out into a protected area was thought to guard them from negative influences, an idea which may have derived from the magician's magical circles. The ceremony of unfolding the cloth at the beginning of a session, and closing the session formally by folding up the cards in the cloth at the end, distinguishes the time set aside for the reading as special.

You will probably want to choose and create your own rituals which will become personal and important to you. For instance, you might prefer to create your own box to keep your cards in rather than use a cloth; or you might choose cloth of any material or colour. What you actually *do* is not important; what does matter is that you forge a ritual for yourself to make the reading something out of the ordinary.

Having created a secure place to do the reading, I shuffle the deck and lay the cards out face down on the silk cloth and invite the seeker to select a number of cards from the face-down pack. You will notice that tarot cards are generally larger than the regular playing deck and may be difficult to handle at first. The Visconti deck is particularly large and may take some practice in learning to shuffle it expertly. Some readers will give the cards to the seeker to shuffle, and ask them to cut the pack before dealing out the cards in the order they appear from the top of the deck. My own preference is to invite the seeker to select a set number of cards from the deck laid out face down, as described above, because although unseen, the cards are, nonetheless, being specifically chosen. The method you choose is, naturally, a matter of personal choice, and you can experiment to see which one suits you best.

Reading Reversed Cards

The question of reading reversed cards would be an appropriate one to address here. A reversed card is one which, when laid out by the seeker, appears upside down. Reading reversed cards is a relatively modern innovation as medieval traditions suggest the cards were interpreted as having the same meanings whichever way up they appeared. According to tarot expert Paul Huson, the idea of reversals came into tarot traditions in France with the advent of Cabbalistic ideas and their theosophical speculations of *Diabolus est Deus Inversus*, 'the Devil is the mirror image of God'. The divinatory meaning for an upright card is, broadly speaking, its opposite when reading it reversed.

As each image has both a positive and negative interpretation available to the seeker, I do not read reversals; I prefer to see both possibilities in the card, whichever way it appears. Reading reversed cards does tend to limit the possible interpretation to upright as positive, and reversed as negative, which I find rather straightjacketing. The divinatory meanings offered in Chapters Two and Three can be looked upon as having both positive and negative meanings, so you can experiment with them and decide whether you like to read reversals or not. There are no hard and fast rules when interpreting the tarot, only guidelines, and it is up to each individual to decide how to interpret them for himself or herself.

Spreads and Case Studies

How you read the cards and the spreads you use is all a matter of taste, and all I can do here is offer you my own personal methods for you to try, adopting or discarding as you feel appropriate. Over the years, I have devised a way of reading which involves three spreads, starting with The Celtic Cross Spread which uses only the Minor Arcana. I use this spread to start off by getting an impression of where a person is in their life, and then move on to The Star Spread which uses only the Major Arcana. This gives an impression of the inner life of the seeker, and the influences upon it which are deep and psychological. For a summary, I mix the Major and Minor Arcana together and lay out The Horseshoe Spread. I will demonstrate these three spreads with a reading for Lucy, giving you my interpretations and responses to her cards as well as her questions and answers. For this I have used the Mythic Tarot.

Further demonstration spreads follow using different packs: The Triangle Spread for Anna using the Morgan-Greer deck, and The Horoscope Spread for Natalie using the Marseilles deck. I will finally give outlines for The Gypsy Draw, The Planetary Deal and The Tree of Life Spread, which will give you further opportunities for experimenting with various layouts before you come to find a routine that makes you feel most comfortable.

Case Study 1
The Celtic Cross Spread

~ An Overview of a Problem ~

Lucy, a 36-year-old woman, married with two children, came for a reading to discuss her position regarding her marriage and family situation. She asked the question 'Are we doing the right thing by not doing anything?' I chose to use the ten-card Celtic Cross Spread using only the cards of the Minor Arcana because I wanted to get a good impression of Lucy's current situation in everyday terms, what the external influences are on her, the mundane circumstances and so on – particularly with regard to her family life. The cards of the Minor Arcana give a good first impression of the seeker as they mirror a detailed picture of ordinary life and can be used effectively to look at specific questions, while those of the Major Arcana reflect a person's psychology and spirituality. Lucy selected the ten cards listed below and laid them out according to the diagram in the order numbered. However, I then read them, for convenience, in the sequence shown by the text; the reasons for this will become apparent as you continue. We used the Mythic Tarot for this reading.

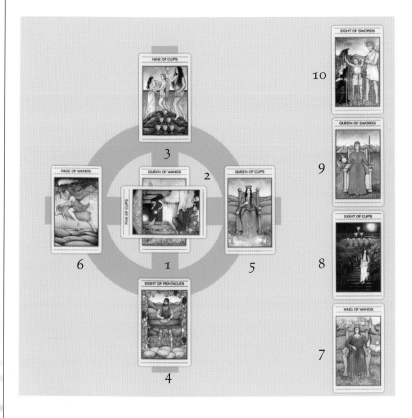

1. *Present Position* – Queen of Wands

2. *What Crosses You* – Five of Cups

3. *What is Above You* – Nine of Cups

4. *What is Below You* – Eight of Pentacles

5. *What is Behind You* – Queen of Cups

6. *What is Before You* – Page of Wands

7. *Your Future Position* – King of Wands

8. *How Others See You* – Eight of Cups

9. *Your Hopes and Fears* – Queen of Swords

10. *The Outcome* – Eight of Swords

| LUCY | *At the moment things are difficult at home. My husband has been relocated at work. His new job is miles away so he has to leave* |

home on Sunday night or terribly early on Monday morning and doesn't get home till Friday, so I am a single mother all week. The children are very demanding and my son really needs his father. The problem is we don't know if this job is going to last and we don't know whether we should relocate and join him. We would have trouble selling this house which we love and the children are well settled in schools here. On the other hand, being apart is putting a great strain on us. My husband feels he needs to prove himself in the job for about six months more before asking for better wages and conditions, but I am finding myself tired and resentful about having all the responsibilities of the house and children on me. I want to ask the cards if there is an alternative or are we doing the right thing by continuing with the situation for a little while longer?

1. Present Position

| JULIET | THE CARD IN POSITION 1. *Present Position* IS THE QUEEN OF WANDS This is an image of the queen of 'Hearth and Home', yet she is quite |

capable of working and running a family too. She represents a woman of energy and enthusiasm – the Wands are the suit of fire which signifies action and energy. In the Mythic Tarot the myth connected with the Queen of Wands is that of Penelope, Queen of Ithaca. When her husband Odysseus was called away to the Trojan War, Penelope was left to rule the island kingdom of Ithaca alone, in addition to looking after their young son Telemaccus.

No fewer than 104 suitors tried to persuade her that her husband would not return, so that they might get their hands on the kingdom. But Penelope was constant and she did not give up hope that Odysseus would return. In order to keep the suitors at bay she gave them hope by announcing that she would marry one of them just as soon as she had finished weaving her father-in-law's funeral shroud. And to ensure that this did not happen, she wove by day under their eagle eyes and unravelled it all by night, so it was never finished. Eventually Odysseus did return.

This myth seems to echo your dilemma, you at home keeping the family together while your husband is away. Perhaps you too have the required energy to cope with the difficult situation you are in. It means you need strength, resolve and determination but, like Penelope, you can do it.

THE CARD IN POSITION 2. *What Crosses You* IS THE FIVE OF CUPS
This position represents what makes life difficult at the moment, what hampers the progress of the card in Position 1, if you like. In your case, the Five of Cups is making the Queen of Wands' job difficult. It is a card which signifies regret over past actions or some sort of disappointment. If you look carefully at the image you can see that four of the five cups have fallen and spilt their contents, but the fifth is still standing upright, and is therefore still full. This symbolizes that although something has gone wrong, nevertheless something remains which is still worth working with.

The image on this card shows the point when Psyche disobeyed her hus-

2. What Crosses You

band, Eros, by trying to find out who he was. She suspected he might be a monster as he only came to her at night. She secretly lit an oil lamp but when she discovered he was, in fact, an extremely attractive god, she fell madly in love with him, her hand trembled and hot oil dripped onto his bare skin and burnt him! He was furious for her treachery and left her. The story goes on to tell that they do manage to overcome their problems, but this is rather a time of uncertainty. Perhaps in your situation it suggests that you may be concentrating too much on the difficulties rather than the opportunities which are available to you.

LUCY *I think that is true. It is a bit of a case of 'Be careful of what you wish for because you might get it!' Before my husband got his new job he was very unhappy at work and also felt very insecure in case he was made redundant. This new position is a definite move in the right direction career wise, and I certainly used to moan that he was not getting anywhere. Now I moan that he is not here to help me!*

JULIET THE CARD IN POSITION 5. *What is Behind You* IS THE QUEEN OF CUPS This position indicates what is passing out of your life – what is no longer working for you at the moment, no longer necessary. The Queen of Cups is an emotional card. Water is a symbol of feelings and this card is an indication of introspection and self-immersion. You can see that the Queen is staring at her reflection in her cup, and her robe is merging into the water at her feet. The Queen of Cups is very absorbed in how she feels. It would appear from its position in the reading – *What is Behind You*, ready to move out of your life – that it may mean the time for feeling sorry for yourself and disappointed in how things have turned out needs to pass. It seems that wallowing in the difficulties of life may not be helping you at the moment. What is relevant in your *Present Position* is the Queen of Wands, the card of optimism and positive, fiery energy.

THE CARD IN POSITION 4. *What is Below You* IS THE EIGHT OF PENTACLES This position represents what is already present in your life, and the Eight of Pentacles is the card of retraining, the card of the apprentice. Have you been doing anything like that lately?

LUCY *Yes, I have recently finished a course in word-processing but I have not found work yet. What I really want is to find a job that will not impinge too much on the children because they need me, but that will enable me to contribute financially, because we are also stressed money wise.*

JULIET THE CARD IN POSITION 3. *What is Above You* IS THE NINE OF CUPS This position describes the influences coming into your life at the moment, and the Nine of Cups is known as the 'wish' card. This means that a wish of paramount importance could be granted to you. It is the card of fulfilling a desire or hope.

5. What is Behind You

4. What is Below You

3. What is Above You

LUCY *Well I would dearly love a job so that at least we would not be so financially stretched and it would also do me good to have somewhere to go during the day when the children are at school. We live in a very isolated place and I can get very lonely which is maybe why I get depressed and down. Of course the problem is that jobs are very few and far between in my area. I did have a part-time job when my husband was still at home and I really liked that but the business folded and I was made redundant.*

JULIET It seems the Five of Cups refers to you mourning the loss of a valued job as well as the change in your marital relationship.

THE CARD IN POSITION 6. *What is Before You* IS THE PAGE OF WANDS
This position refers to what is coming into your life in the near future and the Page of Wands indicates new ideas and the beginnings of something which needs a lot of attention. All the Pages are messengers of new beginnings. The Page of Wands brings creative ideas, and unique ways around difficult situations. You have three fiery cards in your reading which means that the intuitive, creative part of you is being stimulated at the moment. Rather than thinking how problematic everything is, think of it as a challenge to work out what can be done within the limits of your circumstances.

6. What is Before You

LUCY *Yes, you may be right. I am so busy thinking about what has gone wrong and what is troublesome that I am ignoring what I do have that is positive. I used to be very creative before marrying – I painted and wrote a lot. Perhaps I need to take that up again.*

JULIET THE CARD IN POSITION 7. *Your Future Position* IS THE KING OF WANDS
This position represents where you will find yourself in the future. The King of Wands, like his counterpart the Queen, is full of energy, optimism and enthusiasm. He is known as the 'salesman' of the deck. This card represents a very good influence here because it seems as though you are lacking in self-confidence just now, so naturally looking for a new job or getting your creative side started again with that attitude could be difficult. The King of Wands can give you a good push in the right direction though, as his is the sort of energy which makes you feel you can have anything you want if only you try hard and make sure you ask for it. And, of course, if you believe that and go for it, the chances are you will get it!

7. Your Future Position

THE CARD IN POSITION 8. *How Others See You* IS THE EIGHT OF CUPS
This card depicts a figure turning her back on eight neatly stacked cups. It means that no matter how much effort and energy you put into a situation it is no longer viable and a new one has to be sought.

8. How Others See You

LUCY *I can relate to that. I always thought that marriage would mean a settled home and income, children at good schools and family holidays every year. Well it hasn't worked out quite like that and I suppose I am*

not really facing up to it. I don't want to see that things aren't as simple and straightforward as I want them to be.

JULIET   That is right. And perhaps by turning your back on your preconceived ideas and taking a look at what is actually on offer in your marriage, you will find out that there may be more than you think, not less.

THE CARD IN POSITION 9. *Your Hopes and Fears* IS THE QUEEN OF SWORDS
The Queen of Swords is traditionally associated with a woman who has known sorrow but bears her difficulty with dignity. In this position, this card may be showing what you are hoping to achieve. Things are not easy for you just now, but they are not easy for your husband either, nor for the children, as you all miss each other during the week and miss your old life. But you have a lot of influence in the family as the mother and how you handle this difficult situation will have a bearing on how the rest of the family react too.

9. *Your Hopes and Fears*

LUCY   *I must admit I have been complaining a lot about how difficult I am finding things on my own, and how much I have on my shoulders. Perhaps I have been ignoring how difficult it is for John, my husband. I expect he needs me to be a bit more cheerful and supportive rather than whining about what a hard time I am having.*

JULIET   The Queen of Swords may give you the strength to bear these trials with courage and dignity, which in no way detracts from the fact or denies that you are suffering at the moment, but means that you could try to be as constructive as possible given the circumstances.

THE CARD IN POSITION 10. *The Outcome* IS THE EIGHT OF SWORDS
This card signifies a tricky situation: whichever way you turn at the moment there is a problem. For example, staying put and continuing with your husband coming home for weekends feels unsatisfactory because you and the children miss him and he misses you. But, on the other hand, you have a stable home you all like and the children are settled in their schools, so to disrupt them until you are more sure of how your husband's job will turn out would seem a rather rash move. This card is known as the card of 'damned if you do, damned if you don't' but it does signal that a sign will come to show you the way out. Your question was 'Are we doing the right thing by not doing anything?' It seems the answer is that just now you have little choice, but in the near future it will begin to come clear which direction to take.

10. *The Outcome*

LUCY   *That is very encouraging. I am happy to wait a bit to see how things pan out if that seems like the right thing to do. I was worried that I should be forcing some sort of showdown, although I don't know what good that would have done. Perhaps I was just wanting confirmation from the cards that sometimes it is alright to wait something out rather than always trying to force things to happen.*

CASE STUDY 1

THE STAR SPREAD

~ A Closer Look at an Inner Level ~

Lucy was keen to continue and so I suggested we move on to the next stage of my 'structured spread programme'. We then did a seven-card Star Spread for Lucy using only the Major Arcana, again working with the Mythic Tarot. This spread is suitable for trying to work on an inner level as the Major Arcana lends itself well to working on psychological or spiritual issues. In this spread Lucy wanted to concentrate on her personal inner-world development, rather than on her family and other external events, and to think about her own feelings around a job or career. Lucy was sufficiently aware and insightful to realize that blaming her husband and his situation for the dilemma they were in was not the whole story. She had to 'own' the fact that she had issues to resolve herself and that it was no good looking only to external factors to find solutions. Lucy needed to reflect on her own needs and wants as a woman and as an individual rather than hiding behind her role as wife and mother. The cards were drawn as listed below.

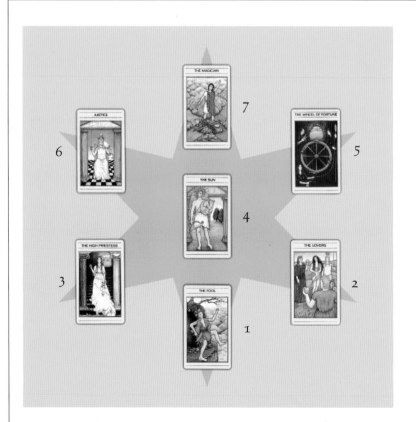

1. *Root of the Matter* – THE FOOL

2. *Feelings, Emotions and Relationships* – THE LOVERS

3. *Thoughts and Career* – THE HIGH PRIESTESS

4. *Heart of the Matter* – THE SUN

5. *What is Surfacing* – THE WHEEL OF FORTUNE

6. *Desires You Have* – JUSTICE

7. *The Outcome* – THE MAGICIAN

JULIET · THE CARD IN POSITION 1. *Root of the Matter* IS THE FOOL
This placement represents the present – what you are thinking about at the moment. The Fool is the card of change and signifies that a shift in attitude is coming. He suggests that old ways need to be discarded and that something new and unknown is coming your way. Perhaps you need to be thinking about what your personal aims and goals should be as well as concentrating on those of your husband.

LUCY · *I have certainly been feeling rather down since I lost my job. It seems I am always starting things but then letting them run through my fingers. The minute things get hard I tend to give up rather than persevere, but to be honest I have always been like that. And, if I am even more honest, I do tend to blame people or things for why I have not been more successful than I am.*

1. *Root of the Matter*

JULIET · Perseverance can certainly be uncomfortable but without it nothing can develop. The Fool here might give you the push you need to start searching for a direction of your own. Perhaps at the moment it is easier for you to concentrate on the difficulties surrounding your husband's job than to address how hard it is for you to decide what *you* want. The Fool suggests that a risk must be taken, you must take a step into something unknown – you see The Fool on the card is standing on the edge of a precipice ready to jump, yet he is optimistic and positive, as if he knows that to move is necessary and that to stay behind is to stagnate.

LUCY · *I can identify with that. I feel as if I am hovering on the edge, not wanting to retreat but too afraid to jump!*

JULIET · THE CARD IN POSITION 2. *Feelings, Emotions and Relationships* IS THE LOVERS
The Lovers is the card which indicates that a choice or decision needs to be made. It is sometimes connected with love affairs or relationships, but always with a trial or choice involved. And whenever we make a choice we are also obliged to relinquish something. In your case, The Lovers seems to represent the need to make a personal decision or choice regarding what you should do and how you want to go about doing it. You are seeking some sort of personal satisfaction, perhaps creatively, intellectually or career wise, as well as trying to find satisfaction within your marriage partnership and family relationships, and perhaps those options seem mutually exclusive.

2. *Feelings, Emotions and Relationships*

LUCY · *That feels right. I feel very torn between wanting to find something which will be important and fulfilling for me to do, and yet wondering whether I am being selfish and not considering the needs of my husband and children. As I said, I used to be quite artistic and I do write well but I allow other things to get in the way, perhaps to avoid getting down to it.*

THE HIGH PRIESTESS

3. Thoughts and Career

THE SUN

4. Heart of the Matter

THE WHEEL OF FORTUNE

5. What is Surfacing

| JULIET | THE CARD IN POSITION 3. *Thoughts and Career* IS THE HIGH PRIESTESS |

The High Priestess is Persephone, goddess of the underworld. Her realm is not of the practical, material world; her rulership is not of the conscious ego but the unconscious mind. When she appears in a reading it means that something is happening under the surface. This card represents a gestation period. It suggests that something important is happening but the process is unconscious, in the same way that during a pregnancy great growth is occurring but in the secret of the womb. What is formed is not visible until the moment of birth. The traditional meaning of The High Priestess is 'secrets revealed but in due course' which means, in other words, that you cannot hurry this process along; it must happen in its own natural time. Because this card falls in the position of *Thoughts and Career*, it seems that some ideas may be 'cooking' inside you with regard to the different directions you could take career or job wise, but they are not quite ready to be acted upon yet. However, just because nothing is visible on the surface does not mean that there is nothing happening at all. Dreams and intuitions are important at the moment too. It is a good idea to allow yourself to play around with ideas and possibilities without feeling the need to pressure yourself. The choices you make with The Lovers do not need to be rushed or forced. They must be allowed to emerge in good time.

THE CARD IN POSITION 4. *Heart of the Matter* IS THE SUN

The Sun sheds some optimistic light on the subject. Whenever The Sun appears in a reading it brings the warmth and clarity of vision which Apollo the sun god was thought to bring to each new day. The Sun can illuminate difficulties and shed light on problems. You may have had the experience of a sleepless night in which you toss and turn and worry in the darkness, feeling quite incapable of making decisions. You may feel anxious and distressed, but as the sun rises and daylight streams through your window you start to feel better, more positive, more optimistic. Suddenly the fears of the night evaporate and things fall into perspective again. The Sun in a reading represents energy and a source of strength.

| LUCY | *That sounds nice and reassuring! I do want to find my old confidence and positive ways of thinking again. I am getting very tired of always feeling down and gloomy.* |

| JULIET | THE CARD IN POSITION 5. *What is Surfacing* IS THE WHEEL OF FORTUNE |

The Wheel of Fortune shows that a new chapter is starting. The wheel is a symbol of both stability and change in oneself. Fate is the moving circumference of the wheel while your true self is at the centre. This card indicates that the more you can be aware of yourself and your own power over your destiny, the clearer things will become and the more influence you will have to turn your fate in the direction you want it to go. In general The Wheel of

Fortune signifies that a new chapter is ready to start, a new run of luck is just beginning, and the more responsibility you take for it, the better and more powerful you will feel.

| LUCY | *I feel as if I am at the lowest point personally so perhaps it is time for me to start climbing up again!* |

| JULIET | Well, there is no reason why not. It seems that the time is approaching for you to turn the corner and start to take some control in your |
life rather than feeling all the power is being taken from you, leaving you with no choice. You do have choices, even though you may not like them much; it important to recognize they exist and work with them as creatively as possible.

| LUCY | *It is true that I do tend to look outwards for solutions rather than seeking them within.* |

6. *Desires You Have*

| JULIET | THE CARD IN POSITION 6. *Desires You Have* IS JUSTICE |
This position indicates what you wish for consciously or what you desire. The Justice card tells us that you want to achieve a clear and balanced way of looking at things. You want to make some decisions and choices for yourself which are not purely emotional but are rational and strategic. Justice suggests there is a need to see things in an objective rather than an emotional way and can help you to find a balance between your emotions and intellect. The scales of Justice shown in the card represent the opposites which must be held in equal balance, both taken fully into consideration, not one sacrificed in favour of the other. You seek to find a balance between your family and their needs and your own needs for personal fulfilment.

THE CARD IN POSITION 7. *The Outcome* IS THE MAGICIAN
This position is the outcome, or 'top of the matter', for this spread. The Magician here offers new scope for intellectual or creative pursuits. There could be a potential opening for work as possibilities are in abundance when this card appears. It will be a time for action and initiative; there may be an upsurge of energy and exciting new opportunities. It seems that once you have absorbed the lessons of the previous cards you will be in a position to fully utilize the promise The Magician always offers.

7. *The Outcome*

| LUCY | *That is very helpful and certainly gives me plenty of food for thought! I am gradually coming to realize how much I need to find* |
something creative and purposeful to do for myself rather than living through my husband and children. Of course I want those things for them but perhaps I have not been fully aware of how much I need them for myself as well. Maybe I am avoiding some of those issues for myself because they are so difficult and it is easier to worry about the family than it is to truly concentrate on my own needs.

CASE STUDY 1

THE HORSESHOE SPREAD

~ The Culmination of the Reading ~

The final stage of this three-part reading is a summary of the first two readings, and for this I select the five-card Horseshoe Spread which uses the whole deck, both the Major and Minor Arcana. It is interesting to note how many of the same cards appear here as in the earlier spreads – in Lucy's case the Page of Wands, the Eight of Swords and The Magician had already appeared in The Celtic Cross and The Star Spreads. It is not unusual for this to happen and it seems as if these cards are in some way particularly significant. In Lucy's case the Page of Wands bringing the seeds of creativity seems very apt, as does the Eight of Swords which perhaps is saying that just because she is unable to find an immediate solution logically does not mean a solution cannot be found. The Magician is particularly significant for Lucy because it connects her with her creativity and that is very important for her sense of personal purpose.

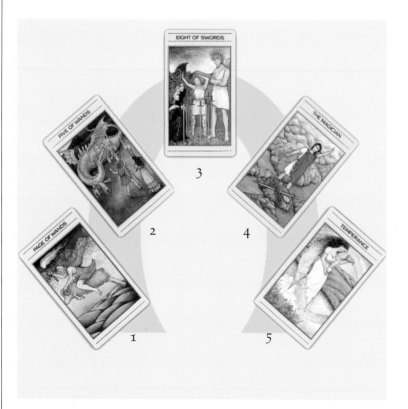

1. *Present Position* – PAGE OF WANDS

2. *The Expected* – FIVE OF WANDS

3. *The Unexpected* – EIGHT OF SWORDS

4. *Near Future* – THE MAGICIAN

5. *Long-term Future* – TEMPERANCE

JULIET THE CARD IN POSITION 1. *Present Position* IS THE PAGE OF WANDS
The Page of Wands in this position echoes the meaning of the same card when it turned up before in The Celtic Cross Spread. The fact that it has made its second appearance serves to emphasize that the spirit of the Page of Wands is very strong for you at the moment. This, of course, means new ideas and creative inspiration, albeit in small ways at first. The Mythic Tarot uses the myth of Phrixus to describe the Page of Wands. The god Zeus gave the boy Phrixus a special ram with a pure-gold fleece and the power to fly, on which he could escape his wicked stepmother. Thus Phrixus brought the Golden Fleece to Colchis. This is the tiny seed without which the great saga of Jason would never have happened. There is clearly a strong desire to move ahead, although the path is yet unclear and your creative ideas, as symbolized by the Page of Wands, just like anything young and fragile, need assistance and nurturing.

JULIET THE CARD IN POSITION 2. *The Expected* IS THE FIVE OF WANDS
This position indicates how you see your life at present and what expectations you have of it, and the Five of Wands suggests a certain amount of tension between reality and fantasy. The image on the card shows Jason fighting with a formidable dragon, which illustrates the point in his journey when he has to really face up to how things are, not how he would like things to be. It is all very well dreaming about capturing the Golden Fleece but the moment has come to actually fight the monster and it is not as easy as he imagined. Perhaps that is how you feel at the moment, in that you would like a nice job which would fit well in your home routine, but finding something like that is not so easy. So, like Jason, you need to find courage and commitment and may need to turn to others for help. Perhaps you need not struggle on your own quite as much as you do.

LUCY *That is true. I do have a tendency to think I have to sort everything out myself and get very despondent when I cannot. I probably could, and should, ask my husband and friends for more help, at least emotionally, but I do hate to feel as though I am burdening others.*

JULIET But you end up feeling burdened yourself and then feel down and depressed and complain about how difficult everything is.

LUCY *Yes, that is true.*

JULIET THE CARD IN POSITION 3. *The Unexpected* IS THE EIGHT OF SWORDS
It is interesting to note that this card has come up again in the position of *The Unexpected*. This is the card of feeling trapped; yet it also carries a message that a sign will come to show you the way. We know you are feeling stuck and uncertain, so perhaps you do not expect a sign to come at all.

PAGE OF WANDS

1. Present Position

FIVE OF WANDS

2. The Expected

EIGHT OF SWORDS

3. The Unexpected

LUCY *Well I certainly cannot think of what would constitute a 'sign'.*

JULIET THE CARD IN POSITION 4. *Near Future* IS THE MAGICIAN
The Magician in this position echoes its position as *The Outcome* in The Star Spread. It seems as though this spread is confirming much of what we spoke about in the first two layouts. The Magician shows potential and possibilities for work and creative pursuits. He stands before a rock on which lie the four emblems of the Minor Arcana, showing that there is plenty to choose from, but you have to make the decisions yourself – use the opportunities that present themselves and be prepared to be quite versatile. Hermes, who is often connected with The Magician, was a very adaptable, resourceful god, always seeking to find ways of turning events to his favour. With his influence so prominent in your cards today it seems that opportunities will crop up and you must be ready for them when they do.

LUCY *I feel, from what you are saying, that what I really need to do is think a bit more optimistically and start to take note of what I have got and can use, rather than wasting so much time worrying about what I do not have. I am sure if I did that more, I would be more able to notice the signs when they appear.*

THE MAGICIAN

4. *Near Future*

JULIET THE CARD IN POSITION 5. *Long-term Future* IS TEMPERANCE
This card offers harmony and moderation for the long term. It has a particularly good influence on marriages and all kinds of partnerships because there is a positive sense of sharing, compromise and give-and-take which is so essential to healthy relationships. The angel on the card is mixing and blending liquid from one cup to the other signifying the constant, flowing exchange of feelings.

LUCY *That is very heartening because I do feel that, although there are difficulties at the moment, my marriage is strong and has the potential to remain stable. And certainly maintaining a good marriage and a happy home life for us all is, when all is said and done, my main priority.*

TEMPERANCE

5. *Long-term Future*

(About 3 months after this reading, Lucy telephoned me to say that a 'sign' had come! Ever since they had lived in that property, Lucy and her husband had been waiting for the house martins to nest on their house as they are both keen bird-watchers, and each year the birds had, after looking as though they might settle, finally gone elsewhere. Now, for the first time, they had made nests and laid eggs, which Lucy had taken as the sign they needed to show that they should stay! She was in the process of making some major renovations to their house as part of their commitment to staying there and felt much more settled. She was following leads on local part-time positions although much of her energy was going into the building works. She had also started painting again.)

CASE STUDY 2
THE TRIANGLE SPREAD
～ A concise and general life picture ～

Anna, a thirty-five-year-old woman, came to see me to get a general picture of what was happening in her life. She had separated from her husband two years previously and had now just started a new job. She did not want to make any big changes but was interested to know how things were in general in the areas of career and love life. Anna had more or less come to terms with the break-up of her marriage and, although she was getting on with her life, she felt the need to know the direction her life was taking. However, as we were short of time, I chose the seven-card Triangle Spread which uses both the Major and Minor Arcana together. This spread is relatively short compared to The Celtic Cross or The Tree of Life Spreads yet quite a lot of information can be gained concisely. We used the Morgan-Greer deck, and the cards were selected as listed below.

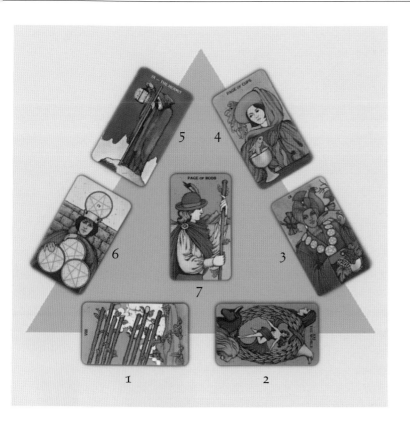

1. AND 2. *Present Position* –
THE EIGHT OF WANDS AND
THE WORLD

3. AND 4. *Immediate Future* –
THE NINE OF PENTACLES AND
THE PAGE OF CUPS

5. AND 6. *Long-term Future* –
THE HERMIT AND
THE FOUR OF PENTACLES

7. *The Overview* –
THE PAGE OF WANDS (RODS)

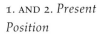

JULIET THE CARDS IN POSITIONS 1. AND 2. *Present Position* ARE THE EIGHT OF WANDS AND THE WORLD

The Eight of Wands and The World representing the current situation mean that things look pretty good. The Eight of Wands signifies a time of plain sailing; if you want to get things done, now would be a good moment to try, as the energy is flowing in the right direction. It is also an indication of a positive mood and generally high spirits. The World symbolizes accomplishment. It would seem that you may have just achieved something you have worked hard for, or realized some kind of goal, perhaps?

ANNA *Yes, that's right, I am very excited about my new job. It is an area which I really wanted to get into and there was a lot of competition, so I feel very pleased that I was finally chosen for the position. I am sure it will prove to be a very interesting job indeed.*

JULIET The World suggests a reward or sense of achievement, which also seems to fit well with what you have just told me, as does the Eight of Wands, the card of energy and enthusiasm.

THE CARDS IN POSITIONS 3. AND 4. *Immediate Future* ARE
THE NINE OF PENTACLES AND THE PAGE OF CUPS

The Nine of Pentacles in this position suggests that you will experience a strong feeling of personal satisfaction and the ability to take pride in the fruits of your own hard labour. You will enjoy your achievements and will be able to appreciate your efforts and feel good about them. The Page of Cups suggests the beginnings of something new in terms of a relationship. Is anything happening on that front?

1. AND 2. *Present Position*

ANNA *No, nothing at the moment. There has been a period of mourning after my husband and I split up. Since then there has been some toing and froing between us but we have finally made a clear decision to split up as amicably as possible. I now feel ready to start thinking about something new.*

JULIET The Page of Cups forecasts new beginnings for your feelings, even though at first they will be delicate, emerging gently.

ANNA *I do feel like that. At first, after the split, I wanted to meet someone else very quickly and began to think I never would. Now I feel very happy with my own company and I know that, while I would ideally like to meet someone, it is not the end of the world if I don't. I am really happy being on my own which I never used to be.*

3. AND 4.
Immediate Future

JULIET Perhaps you are already feeling the influence of the Nine of Pentacles which is connected with solitary enjoyment of life. It does not mean you have to be alone, just that you have the capacity for it.

THE CARDS IN POSITIONS 5. AND 6. *Long-term Future* ARE THE HERMIT AND THE FOUR OF PENTACLES

The Hermit suggests that an inner journey will become appropriate, reflecting a need to get to know yourself better, which will include coming to terms with time and its limitations. The Hermit teaches you to feel your way through things rather than charging through life like a bull in a china shop. It represents a profound change in attitude as you become more reflective and contemplative.

ANNA *That is interesting and accurate. Until the split with my husband I was never on my own, and at first I couldn't stand it. I was always out or had people round, anything not to be alone. Things have gradually changed and now I can actually enjoy having time on my own to read, think or do whatever I like. It has been a great learning experience. Are you are saying this experience will continue?*

JULIET Yes, it seems this card will be important. If you can survive being alone you need never fear it. The Hermit also teaches patience and that hurried decisions can be costly in the long term.

ANNA *That is certainly true. I rushed into my marriage – we met and married in less than a year. I will never do that again.*

JULIET The Four of Pentacles warns that you must beware getting stuck in a situation and feeling too scared to take risks. It signifies a fear of letting go, a fear, perhaps, of upsetting the status quo?

ANNA *We are coming up to the time when we could get divorced. I want to go through with it, and yet I am also afraid to make the final break.*

JULIET Certainly, letting go of your marriage – even though you no longer want it – may feel like a risk. There is a security in being married, even though you no longer live together, and it might be difficult to completely clear the decks. The Four of Pentacles suggests a tendency to hold back.

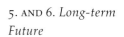

THE CARD IN POSITION 7. *The Overview* IS THE PAGE OF WANDS (RODS)

The Page of Wands suggests creativity and new ideas. This is not necessarily artistic creativity, but rather allowing your imagination freedom to create new ideas and ways of doing things. In this position it indicates that a creative spark may catch light and produce quite a blaze! Remember that all the Pages represent the tiny beginnings from which great things may emerge.

Taking the reading as a whole, now seems to be a time of great energy and excitement in your life, with good potential for career and relationships, and also for work on an inner level.

ANNA *That sounds good and also it fits with how I feel about my life at the moment.*

5. AND 6. *Long-term Future*

7. *The Overview*

CASE STUDY 3
THE HOROSCOPE SPREAD

~ A detailed view of a situation in the present ~

Natasha, a thirty-year-old woman who had been living abroad for ten years, had recently returned to her home country to do a course in alternative healing. She was, however, feeling unsettled and rather depressed about the move which was not as easy as she had hoped and wanted a reading to look at all aspects of her life. As she was both interested in astrology and wanted an overview of her current situation rather than to ask a specific question, I chose The Horoscope Spread which is a twelve-card spread using both the Major and Minor Arcana, with each card representing a house of the zodiac. Natasha selected twelve cards from the Marseilles deck and laid them out in a circle. The cards chosen are listed below.

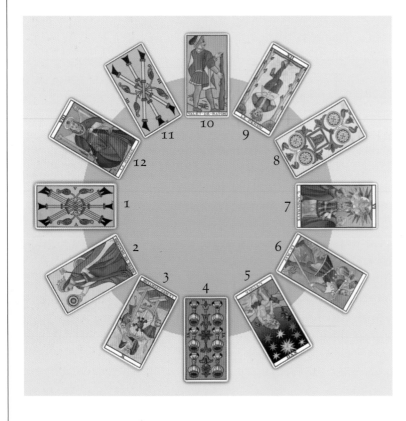

1. (FIRST HOUSE) *Self* – FIVE OF WANDS
2. (SECOND HOUSE) *Values* – QUEEN OF PENTACLES
3. (THIRD HOUSE) *Communication* – THE WHEEL OF FORTUNE
4. (FOURTH HOUSE) *Home* – SIX OF CUPS
5. (FIFTH HOUSE) *Creativity* – THE STAR
6. (SIXTH HOUSE) *Work* – THE FOOL
7. (SEVENTH HOUSE) *Relationships* – THE LOVERS
8. (EIGHTH HOUSE) *Transformation* – FOUR OF PENTACLES
9. (NINTH HOUSE) *Spirituality and Higher Aims* – THE HANGED MAN
10. (TENTH HOUSE) *Career and Status* – PAGE OF WANDS
11. (ELEVENTH HOUSE) *Groups and Friends* – THREE OF WANDS
12. (TWELFTH HOUSE) *Unconscious* – JUSTICE

| JULIET | THE CARD IN THE FIRST HOUSE *Self* IS THE FIVE OF WANDS

This house represents you and how you experience the world. The Five of Wands here signifies a battle, or even a collision, between reality and vision. It is your dreams and imagination clashing with mundane reality. In the First House, it suggests that your ideas of the way things should be may be getting a bit of a battering by the reality of how things are.

| NATASHA | *I would say that is true in the extreme! I returned to this country with high hopes after having been away for a long time, only to be faced with the grim reality that the things I wanted to leave behind all those years ago are still here and just as bad. I must admit that it all feels very bleak. I had a lot of dreams when I lived abroad. I had a great deal to look forward to and felt optimistic about my life; but back here I suddenly find it very difficult to live out my ambitions. All the same, I knew I needed to come back to face some things, including family issues, which I left unfinished nearly ten years ago.*

| JULIET | So when you were away you found it easier to imagine that things would be different back home than to face up to the reality now that you are here again?

1. Self

| NATASHA | *Yes, I knew intellectually it would be hard but I don't think I had allowed myself to imagine just how hard! Now that I am here, the truth is stark – the difficulties are confronting me right in the face. I feel that I have lost my dreams. It is a real anticlimax.*

| JULIET | THE CARD IN THE SECOND HOUSE *Values* IS THE QUEEN OF PENTACLES

The Queen of Pentacles in this position is about your body and your physical circumstances, and the importance for you to be looking after and paying attention to your needs in that area. Taking good care of yourself is not an indulgence but a necessity. The Queen's message is that you should be trying to meet all of your needs and as many of your wants as possible. Many people fear this will make them spoilt or greedy, yet in reality it has the effect of making them feel satisfied and comfortable – which ultimately makes them feel generous to others and generally nicer to be around. This is an earthy card, a Taurus in astrology, and therefore anything to do with the senses is important. Taurus rules the Second House which adds further emphasis.

2. Values

| NATASHA | *I suppose I am quite bad at that sort of thing. Although I exercise and eat carefully it is really difficult for me to give myself what I consider to be luxuries.*

| JULIET | THE CARD IN THE THIRD HOUSE *Communication* IS THE WHEEL OF FORTUNE

This position signifies communication and education, and The Wheel of Fortune suggests that something new is opening out. Because this card is a

3. Communication

Major Arcana, its effect is particularly profound. The way you think, and the way you communicate what you think, is changing. Also the course you are taking must be stimulating your mind and providing you with new food for thought.

NATASHA *Actually, I am experiencing some difficulty communicating with people just now because I am still abroad in my heart and mind. I am having real trouble letting go of the friends and way of life I left and am deliberately being reclusive at the moment. I suppose this will have to change if I am to accomplish what I came here for. Also, the course I am studying is more difficult than I had bargained for and I feel that I don't fit in too well with the other students.*

JULIET While you are still reluctant to finally close the chapter on your old life, it will obviously be more difficult to open up the new one which is indicated by this card. You have gone through the motions of change by physically moving but, emotionally, you have not accepted the change and so you are not really 'here'. The Wheel of Fortune in this position is likely to help you with that transition.

4. *Home*

THE CARD IN THE FOURTH HOUSE *Home* IS THE SIX OF CUPS

The Six of Cups is a card of nostalgia in the position of your home and roots. It may describe how you are feeling about the country, friends and home you have left. It may also suggest that something important from your past will need sorting out now.

NATASHA *I think both are right. I do feel as though I am mourning the loss of my friends and where I lived for so long, yet I knew I had to come back here to finish things off. I never said goodbye when I left here, I just pulled away abruptly and never really finished anything. And, although I loved where I was living abroad and had great friends, I knew that one day I would have to come back here and finish things properly. I think I always knew it was inevitable.*

JULIET So the Six of Cups in the position of *Home* signifies your going back and facing something from the past in order to deal with it in the present.

5. *Creativity*

THE CARD IN THE FIFTH HOUSE *Creativity* IS THE STAR

The Fifth House, *Creativity*, is the position of love affairs, romance, the place where you 'play' and enjoy yourself. The Star is a positive card which signifies hope. So no matter how bad things get, and how down in the dumps you feel, it provides you with enough optimism to keep you going. Although just now you may be feeling bleak, The Star shines out to remind you that there is something hopeful to work for out there, even though you may find it difficult to see the bright side at the moment. This card represents a point of light in the darkness and something to be guided by even though you are still uncertain about where you are going.

| NATASHA | *Yes, I do know that somewhere alongside my depressed feelings I have a sense of hope that things will improve. Perhaps that is why I came to see you.* |

| JULIET | THE CARD IN THE SIXTH HOUSE *Work* IS THE FOOL |

In the house of work and service, The Fool suggests that a leap into the unknown has been taken or may be about to be taken. It may also look 'foolish' to those around you.

| NATASHA | *Well that certainly fits in terms of my work, because I have recently taken a part-time job working for a railway company in order to fit in with my course. Without a doubt, it is quite different from the work I did before – I was a teacher. However, I decided when I came to this country that I wanted something quite different, so I took this job which I actually find quite enjoyable. It makes a big change from my healing course – in fact it could not be more opposite really, so I suppose that may seem 'foolish' to some people.* |

6. Work

| JULIET | THE CARD IN THE SEVENTH HOUSE *Relationships* IS THE LOVERS |

The Lovers suggests that you may have choices to make in the area of relationships – whether personal or business.

| NATASHA | *At the moment I am conscious of how very 'choosy' I feel about relationships. Before, I used to try to make friends with anybody and everybody – anything rather than be lonely – but now I feel very differently. I really want to choose who I spend time with and for what purpose. I guess this is because I am no longer afraid of being alone.* |

| JULIET | THE CARD IN THE EIGHTH HOUSE *Transformation* IS THE FOUR OF PENTACLES |

7. Relationships

This is the house of the underworld, and is connected with death, rebirth, transformation and sex. The Four of Pentacles is known as the card of the miser, which means there may be a strong resistance to letting anything go. In this placing, it would seem that there is quite a fear of letting go in close or intimate relationships. In the Seventh House relationships may range from casual acquaintances to love affairs, but the Eighth House suggests very deep and profound connections with others. Perhaps you are hanging on to things for fear of taking a risk with something vulnerable and personal.

| NATASHA | *I don't have a good track record with relationships. I always seem to be the one who wants the relationship more than the other. I have become so fed up with feeling weakened and diminished that I tend to go the other way now and clam up.* |

8. Transformation

JULIET That might be what the Four of Pentacles is signifying; that is, that you constantly frustrate yourself by refusing relationships because you are so afraid of being hurt.

NATASHA *It is true that I do have a fear of intimacy. I think my way of coping with it is by choosing partners who can't give me what I want and then I can blame them.*

JULIET THE CARD IN THE NINTH HOUSE *Spirituality and Higher Aims* IS THE HANGED MAN

The Ninth House is the position of aspirations and longing for knowledge of higher things. The Hanged Man stands for sacrifice, giving something up in order to obtain something you want more. The message of this card is not as simple as merely swapping one thing for another – it calls for a bit of faith on your part. You are required to give something up and, although you hope to get something more meaningful in return, there is no guarantee.

9. Spirituality and
Higher Aims

NATASHA *It feels like that is what I did by coming back. I had to give up everything I had worked at for ten years – a place to live, friends and work – and face the unknown by going back to where I started. And yes, I do hope, and deep down I believe, that I will gain more than I have lost. I can believe that some of the time, and somewhere inside, I really do have faith in myself, only right now things do not feel very positive.*

JULIET It is important to remember that The Hanged Man suggests a conscious or deliberate choice. In your case you chose to try to improve something in your life on an inner level rather than a materially motivated one. Everything has its price and now you are having to pay for the consequences of that choice. However, if you can bear it and keep following the path you have chosen, you might well be pleased with the result of your labours.

THE CARD IN THE TENTH HOUSE *Career and Status* IS THE PAGE OF WANDS
The Page of Wands represents a tiny spark of fire which can turn into a mighty blaze if it is properly stoked and fanned. Just as a huge pile of wood needs only a little flame to turn it into a bonfire, so can great things emerge in the creative and imaginative realm from just a small idea. Because this card is in the house of your career or position in the world it probably reflects something that will be taking place in the work arena.

10. Career and Status

NATASHA *At the moment I do not know where my career will take me. I certainly do not plan to carry on doing what I do now forever, but I am not sure what I really want either. The study course I am taking now is good but, again, I am not sure if it is what I ultimately want. I suppose what you are saying is that I should not be too quick to dismiss any new ideas.*

JULIET That's right. Lots of ideas may come to you, and one or two of them may eventually take root. You came here to do a particular course and now you are wondering if that course is really the direction you want to go in. Well, maybe it is acting as a catalyst, something which propels you in a certain direction from which you can branch off to something else that you would never have thought of had you not done the course. Sometimes life takes us on rather roundabout routes, without which we would never discover things we really need to learn. Again we hear the message of The Hanged Man showing that we have to make sacrifices and sometimes let go of our desire to control life and simply follow its lead.

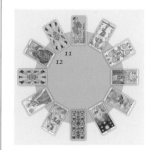

THE CARD IN THE ELEVENTH HOUSE *Groups and Friends* IS THE
THREE OF WANDS
This card indicates that you have reached a stage of initial completion but find there is still much to accomplish. What you thought would be the end turns out to be the beginning, which you can see now that the first stages are in place.

NATASHA *Yes, that is true. When I was abroad, I felt that once I was on the course and back here, everything would be sorted out. Now I am here I realize it is not quite that easy. I am home again which is difficult and the course is fine, although not as easy as I had expected. It is beginning to dawn on me that I am going to have to work hard.*

11. Groups and Friends

JULIET The Three of Wands presents a wonderfully ambivalent image. It shows a completion but only of the first stage from which so much needs to spring. It is disappointing at first to realize that what you thought was the end is, in fact, the beginning; yet, on the other hand, there is so much potential and opportunity on the horizon before you that it can also be an exciting and interesting time.

THE CARD IN THE TWELFTH HOUSE *Unconsciousness* IS JUSTICE
The twelfth house is the mysterious house of the unconscious and hidden, secret things. The card of Justice in this position signals a need for some clarity of vision in this area. It symbolizes the need to understand things rationally, through the intellect. Perhaps some of the emotional issues that brought you back to this country – your family, for example – need to be clearly understood and rationally thought through. It sounds as if you left your home country many years ago and so suddenly for emotional rather than rational reasons. Now you have come full circle and need to understand why.

12. Unconsciousness

NATASHA *That is true and actually feels very appropriate. It is what I need to work on, and I do plan to do just that. I think it has been very helpful to see so much of what is happening in my life at the moment mapped out in the card images.*

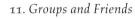

FURTHER SPREADS

The following spreads are provided for you to experiment with further. They vary in complexity: the first two are quite simple and good for starting off with. As you become more experienced you can attempt the more difficult spreads like The Tree of Life.

The Gypsy Draw

This simple three-card layout is a good one to practise on when you first start doing readings. Both the Major and Minor Arcana are used for this spread. The seeker chooses three cards and lays them out from left to right. The first card indicates the seeker and the position he or she is in; the second and third cards represent the situations and people he or she is about to encounter respectively.

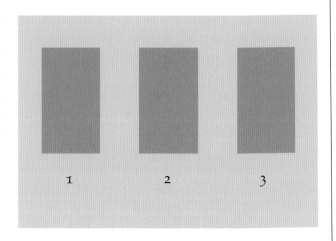

1. *The Seeker*
2. *The Situation You Are About to Encounter*
3. *The People You Are About to Encounter*

The Planets Spread

Here, eight cards are selected from the whole deck, one to represent the seeker and one for each of the seven astrological planets of antiquity. The cards are laid in a circle with the eighth card in the middle. The cards should then be read in pairs – The Moon contrasted with The Sun, Venus with Mars, Jupiter with Saturn. When anything arises which seems incompatible or irreconcilable, the answer will lie in the position of Mercury, the reconciler.

This spread can also be used to give a weekly review, reading the cards from Sunday to Saturday.

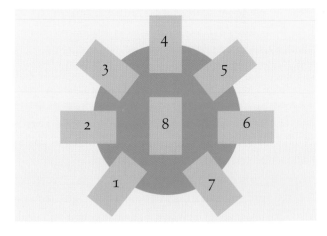

1. (THE MOON) *Home Life, Domestic Matters and Emotional States*
2. (THE SUN) *Achievement, Personal Reward and Optimism*
3. (MERCURY) *Working Life, Career Prospects and Mental Abilities*

4. (VENUS) *Love Life, Relationships and Feelings*
5. (MARS) *Conflict and Struggles*
6. (JUPITER) *Gain and Expansion*
7. (SATURN) *Restriction and Structure*
8. *The Seeker*

The Tree of Life Spread

This spread lays out ten cards in the pattern of the Tree of Life (*see pages 8–9*), using both the Major and Minor Arcana. The cards can be read from Kether down to Malkuth from right to left. Or, alternatively, the path can be followed in reverse from Malkuth to Kether, like the ascending steps of a spiritual staircase. Reading from Kether to Malkuth, the Tree of Life shows the path which leads spirit to matter; from Malkuth upwards it reveals the steps man must negotiate to reach spiritual understanding. Finally, this spread can also be read from a more mundane viewpoint by using the meanings 'Initiative', 'Limitations', 'Gains', and so on for each card.

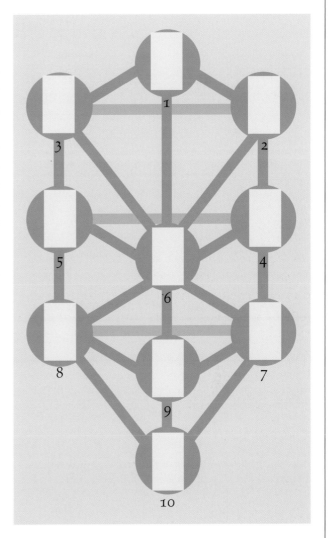

1. (Kether) *The Spiritual Path or Quest of the Seeker*
2. (Hokmah) *Wisdom and Personal Initiative*
3. (Binah) *Understanding and Limitations*
4. (Hesed) *Grace, Mercy and Gains*
5. (Geburah) *Power and Severity*
6. (Tifereth) *Beauty, Glory and Harmony*
7. (Netsah) *Endurance, Victory and Emotion*
8. (Hod) *Majesty, Intellect and Communication*
9. (Yesod) *Foundation and Health*
10. (Malkuth) *Kingdom and Home*

FURTHER READING

Campbell, Joseph. *The Masks of God: Oriental Mythology*. London: Penguin, 1992. New York: Viking Penguin, 1970

Cavendish, Richard. *The Tarot*. London: Michael Joseph, 1975

Cavendish, Richard. *King Arthur and the Grail*. London: Weidenfeld & Nicolson, 1978

Douglas, Alfred. *The Tarot*. London: Penguin, 1972. New York: Penguin, 1992

Graves, Robert. *The Greek Myths*. London: Penguin, 1992. New York: Penguin, 1993

Gray, Eden. *The Tarot Revealed*. London: Bantam, 1969. New York: Signet, 1969

Huson, Paul. *The Devil's Picturebook*. London: Abacus, 1972

Kaplan, Stuart R. *The Encyclopedia of Tarot Volumes I, II and III*. Stamford, CA: US Games Systems Inc., 1978

Kaplan, Stuart R. *The Tarot of the Witches Book*. Stamford, CA: U.S. Games Systems Inc., 1986

Kenton, Warren. *The Anatomy of Fate*. London: Rider, 1978

McCormack, Kathleen. *Tarot*. London: Fontana, 1973

Neumann, Erich. *Amor & Pyche*. Princeton, New Jersey: Princeton University Press, 1992

Pollack, Rachel. *The Haindl Tarot Volmues I and II*. North Hollywood, CA: Newcastle Publishing Company, 1990

Pollack, Rachel. *The New Tarot*. London: The Aquarian Press, 1989. Woodstock, NY: Overlook, 1992

Pollack, Rachel. *The Seventy-eight Degrees of Wisdom, Parts One and Two*. London: The Aquarian Press, 1980

Riley, Jana. *Tarot Dictionary and Compendium*. Stamford, CA: U.S. Games Systems Inc., 1997

Sharman-Burke, Juliet and Liz Greene. *The Mythic Tarot*. London: Rider, 1986

Sharman-Burke, Juliet. *The Mythic Tarot Workbook*. London: Rider, 1989. New York: Fireside, 1988

Sharman-Burke, Juliet. *The Complete Book of Tarot*. New York: St. Martin's Press, 1996

Yates, Frances A. *The Art of Memory*. London: Pimlico, 1992. Chicago: University of Chicago Press, 1974

USEFUL CONTACTS AND ADDRESSES

THE CENTRE FOR PSYCHOLOGICAL ASTROLOGY
For information on tarot courses contact the Centre for Psychological Astrology at:
BCM Box 1815, London WC1N 3XX, UK.
Tel. 0181 749 2330

U.S. GAMES SYSTEMS
U.S. Games Systems was founded in 1968 by Stuart R. Kaplan. It markets approximately 850 items from over twenty product categories comprising tarot, playing cards, family and children's card games, books, speciality advertising products and educational and motivational playing cards.

It exports to twenty countries and sells to almost 8,000 accounts – primarily bookstores, book clubs, book distributors, gift shops including museum gift shops and department store gift departments, greeting card stores, toy and game stores, hobby shops and mail order catalogues.

U.S. Games Systems develops up to twenty new products annually and each product is targeted to support its continued penetration of a variety of 'niche' markets – smaller, special-interest, quality-conscious consumer segments. The overall product line is characterized by the high quality of illustrations, photography and colour and card or paper stock. Some of their most popular tarot products include Rider-Waite, Crowley, Universal Waite, Cat People, Motherpeace, Medicine Woman, Aquarian, Morgan-Greer, Londa and Native American.

U.S. Games Systems has received many awards, such as Mensa Best Mind Games Award, Games Magazine Best 100, Parents Council Awards, and Company of the Year Award from the Stamford Chamber of Commerce.

U.S. Games Systems may be reached at:
179 Ludlow Street, Stamford, CT 06902 USA.
Tel. 203-353-8400
Fax. 203-353-8431
e-mail: USGames@aol.com
website: http://members.aol.com/usgames/index.html

The Fournier Collection is the world's finest and most extensive collection of playing cards, currently consisting of some 15,000 decks dating back as far as the fourteenth century. The Fournier Playing Card Museum of Alava houses the collection in the Bendaña Palace in medieval Vitoria-Gasteiz, and its essential goals are research, conservation and exhibition.

The Fournier Playing Card Museum may be reached at:
Cuchillería, 54, 01001 Vitoria-Gasteiz, Spain

APPENDIX
Notes on the decks used in this book

Illustrations from El Grand Tarot Esoterico reproduced by permission of Naipes Heraclio Fournier S. A.

Illustrations from Le Tarot de Marseilles reproduced by permission of Naipes Heraclio Fournier S. A.

Illustrations from the Haindl Tarot Deck reproduced by permission of Droemersche Verlagsanstalt Th.Knaur, München. Copyright © 1988 by Droemersche Verlagsanstalt Th.Knaur, München. Further reproduction prohibited.

Illustrations from The Norse Tarot Deck reproduced by permission of HarperCollins Publishers Limited, London. Copyright © Clive Barrett 1989. Further reproduction prohibited.

Illustrations from the Swiss 1JJ Tarot reproduced by permission of AGM AGMÜLLER, Bahnhofstrasse 21, CH-8212 Neuhausen am Rheinfall, Switzerland. Copyright © AGM AGMÜLLER. Further reproduction prohibited.

Illustrations from the Rider-Waite Tarot Deck are copyright, and are reproduced (except in the USA) by permission of Rider Books, 20 Vauxhall Bridge Road, London, SW1V 2SA. Further reproduction prohibited.

Illustrations reproduced from The Mythic Tarot (Eddison Sadd Editions). Published by Rider (UK), Fireside (USA), Stoddart (Can) and Simon and Schuster (ANZ).

Illustrations from the Visconti Sforza Tarocchi Deck reproduced by permission of U.S. Games Systems, Inc., Stamford, CT 06902 USA. Copyright © 1975 by U.S. Games Systems, Inc. Further reproduction prohibited.

Illustrations from the Morgan-Greer Tarot Deck reproduced by permission of U.S. Games Systems, Inc., Stamford, CT 06902 USA. Copyright © 1979 by U.S. Games Systems, Inc. Further reproduction prohibited.

Illustrations from the Ukiyoe Tarot Deck reproduced by permission of U.S. Games Systems, Inc., Stamford, CT 06902 USA. Copyright © 1982 by U.S. Games Systems, Inc. Further reproduction prohibited.

Illustrations from the Russian Tarot of St. Petersburg Deck reproduced by permission of U.S. Games Systems, Inc., Stamford, CT 06902 USA. Copyright © 1992 by U.S. Games Systems, Inc. Further reproduction prohibited.

Illustrations from the Tarot of the Witches Deck reproduced by permission of U.S. Games Systems, Inc., Stamford, CT 06902 USA. Copyright © 1983 by U.S. Games Systems, Inc. Further reproduction prohibited.

Illustrations from the Rider-Waite Tarot Deck reproduced (except in the UK) by permission of U.S. Games Systems, Inc., Stamford, CT 06902 USA. Copyright © 1971 by U.S. Games Systems, Inc. Further reproduction prohibited.

INDEX

Page numbers in *italics* refer to illustrations

Acknowledgements

To all those whose excellent books and decks provided so much inspiration for this one. Many thanks to the Eddison Sadd team – Ian, Nick, Zoë, Sarah and Sophie – and to Barbara Levy for all her help.

EDDISON•SADD EDITIONS

Editorial Director	Ian Jackson
Editor	Sophie Bevan
Proofreader	Michele Turney
Indexer	Dorothy Frame
Art Director	Elaine Partington
Senior Art Editor	Sarah Howerd
Chapter-opener Illustrator	Richart Earley
Production	Karyn Claridge and Charles James